BIG BLUES FROM TEXAS
STEVIE RAY VAUGHAN

An In-depth Look at His Powerhouse Guitar Style
Featuring Transcriptions and Lessons

by Dave Rubin

Cover Photo by Lisa Seifert/STAR FILE

ISBN 0-7935-6040-3

7777 W. BLUEMOUND RD. P.O. BOX 13819 MILWAUKEE, WI 53213

INTRODUCTION

Stevie Ray Vaughan did not burst upon the blues scene in 1983, he exploded out of it. At a time when a blues guitar hero like Buddy Guy was looking for a record company and Johnny Winter was reeling from the recent death of his mentor, Muddy Waters, Stevie Ray's big, bad Strat had a galvanizing impact on guitarists. He possessed incredible chops, a monstrous Texas-sized tone, and a penchant for *accurately* covering Jimi Hendrix. As the rock world was slouching towards synth-driven pop, Stevie Ray made his statement the old fashioned way with the relatively unadorned electric guitar. He played the real deal blues, derived from his idols, but filtered through his own brawny, high energy sensibilities. He played his axe for all he was worth, all the time, like a man obsessed. His older brother Jimmie, a masterful guitarist in his own right, used to say that Stevie always sounded like he was "busting out of jail." Blues and rock guitarists rejoiced as he ran roughshod through the music community for the next four years.

Stevie Ray was the state-of-the art Texas blues guitarist in the eighties, and the latest link in the chain of lineage that stretched back to the immortal T-Bone Walker. Coincidentally, Stevie was born in Oak Cliff, Texas, a suburb of Dallas, as was the mighty T-Bone. With brother Jimmie functioning as guitar guru, the Hoo Doo magic of electric blues, R&B and jazz were revealed. The power and glory of Lonnie Mack, Albert King, Buddy Guy, Charlie Christian, and Kenny Burrell pulsed through the Vaughan household, with the siren song of Jimi Hendrix's Voo Doo blues providing the persona and axe of choice. The shuffles of Jimmy Reed, the stinging leads of B.B. and Freddie King, as well as the flashing virtuosity of the great gypsy jazz guitarist, Django Reinhardt, were also absorbed and employed to spectacular effect.

By looking at a selection of tunes from the five studio albums (Note: *The Sky Is Crying* was posthumously released) we can clearly see how Stevie Ray transformed his influences into a remarkably rich and varied guitar style. Lightning leads, full driving rhythmic accompaniment, and tasty, logical fills abound for your musical delectation. They can be a door into your own creativity and a fitting tribute to Stevie Ray Vaughan's lasting legacy.

TEXAS FLOOD
Epic records BFE 38734, (1983)

Texas Flood was originally recorded in Jackson Browne's studio as a demo. Browne had heard, met and played with Stevie Ray at the Montreaux Jazz Festival in Switzerland in 1982. The tape was presented to legendary jazz, R&B and rock producer John Hammond, Sr., who purchased it and brokered a deal at Epic Records.

The debut LP of Stevie Ray Vaughan and Double Trouble gave full exposure to Stevie Ray's awesome chops while offering a tantalizing peek at his future potential. The covers ranged from major domo Buddy Guy's "Mary Had a Little Lamb" to the South Side blues of Howlin' Wolf's "Tell Me," Larry Davis's slow blues classic, "Texas Flood," and a blisteringly fast instrumental remake of the Parliaments' "I Wanna Testify."

From the six originals, I have chosen "Love Struck Baby," "Pride and Joy," "Rude Mood," and the Hendrixian ballad "Lenny" as being representative of Stevie Ray's development to date.

Be aware that, like Hendrix, Stevie Ray tuned his guitar a half step below concert pitch. Inasmuch as he used steel cables gauged .013-.056, this lessening of tension may have eased the strain on both his hands and vocal chords! At any rate, this tuning system will be given before each song even though the actual notation will be at concert pitch. After you have the fingerings worked out and memorized, you may want to detune your axe so that you can shadow Stevie's hot licks.

BIG BLUES FROM TEXAS
STEVIE RAY VAUGHAN
CONTENTS

LOVE STRUCK BABY
(Texas Flood)
Words and Music by Stevie Ray Vaughan

Though known world wide as a heavy electric bluesman, Stevie Ray Vaughan could rock the house with pile driving, pumping rock 'n' roll. "Love Struck Baby" is a prime cut of vintage fifties rockabilly, served up with spanking Strat-tone, butt-kicking boogie rhythms and slicked back, ducktailed vocals. Eddie Cochran, Chuck Berry, and Brian Setzer would be proud!

In the grand rock 'n' roll tradition, *Texas Flood* opens with a hard-driving single; "Love Struck Baby" breaks out of the chute headed for the Top 100. It may not have made it, but the energy of this 2:19 scorcher could have blown away every au courant, pop rock poseur of the era, with their mod clothes and wimpy surf guitars.

Figure 1 Study

The solo in "Love Struck Baby" is so *bad* that I have included all three romping, stomping 12-bar choruses. In this knucklebusting wrist twister, Stevie Ray lets his Strat lecture us with a mini-history of fifties rock 'n' roll.

The first chorus (A) starts with Chuck Berry style double-stops in fourths, followed by a bent diminished chord nicked from T-Bone Walker. The Chuckster was heavily influenced by 'Bone, as well as the jump blues of Louis Jordan, country & western music, and the electric Delta blues of Elmore James.

More Walker-derived Berryisms pop up next with the classic "G string bent against the dyad on the top two strings" taking the solo to the IV chord, as is done in the next two choruses as well. Stevie Ray injects a series of Chuck's dyads in fourths and thirds, combined with the G-string bend, over the V chord in measures 9 and 10. Measures 11 and 12 contain A and E triple-stops and chords.

Chorus #2 (B) begins with the brutal bending and mashing of the A° (diminished) chord, which leads to a breathtaking series of 6/9 chords (beloved by rockabilly cats) climbing chromatically from the I to the IV chord. Freddie King's "Hideaway" 9th chord (which he borrowed from Robert Lockwood, Jr.) sparkles and shimmers for the next two measures of the I chord. The last four measures basically recap those of the first chorus.

The third chorus (C) is a chordal knockout, with Stevie Ray comping 9th chords like a deranged swing guitarist caught in a time warp with Bill Haley's Comets. After easing (?) out of the chord welter in measure 33 by cracking the dyads in fourths with a smart G-string bend, he cascades down the blues scale with fourths and thirds in a manner similar to choruses 1 and 2. Triple-stop A and E7 harmonies close out this opus de cool.

Figure 1 Performance

Clean, logical fingerings are the key to this chordal information highway. The double and triple stops in measures 1, 4, 5, 6, 8, 9, and 10 can be facilitated by firmly anchoring the index finger to the top two strings at fret 5. The same holds true for measures 20, 21, 22, and 24, and measures 32-36.

The A° diminished chord should be played with the second finger on the G string, the index finger on the B string, and the ring finger on the high E string. If you are able to keep your thumb hooked over the edge of the neck while you hold the chord shape, you will find it much easier to bend the notes the required quarter and half steps.

The ultra groovy 6/9 chords work best if the ring finger holds down the high E and B strings, while the index finger manages the D and G strings. The A9 "Freddie King chord" in measures 18 and 19 and measures 25-31 should be fingered thusly: ring finger = D string; second finger = G string; index finger = B string; and pinky = high E string. In the lower positions on the neck this chord can be a tendon stretcher, but at the 17th fret you should be able to reach it in your sleep!

All of the chord forms and shapes in this solo are excellent for fattening up the sound of blues, blues/rock, swing blues, R&B, rockabilly, and roots rock 'n' roll (whew!). In addition, the double-stops provide blues power when you desire scalar motion, and when single note lines would sound thin. And let us not forget that bent diminished chord. It has a handsome history—going back to the swing era when horn sections would often gliss up and down on chords imitating a train whistle. T-Bone and Chuck Berry loved it as a spicy accent and it lives on today in the work of neo-swing pickers like Duke Robillard, Little Charlie Baty, Junior Watson, Ronnie Earl, and Brian Setzer.

Figure 1

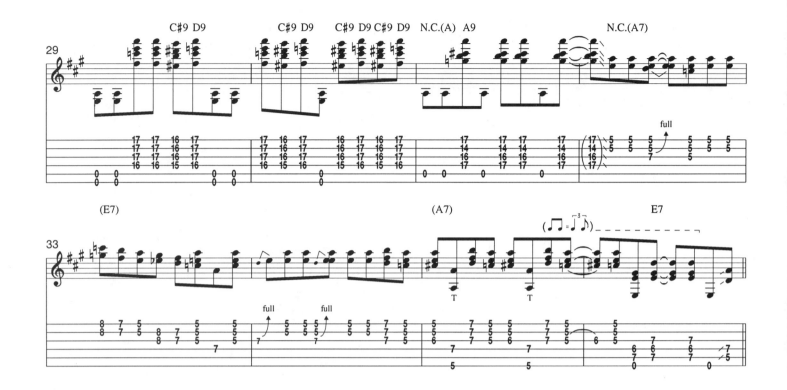

PRIDE AND JOY
(Texas Flood)
Words and Music by Stevie Ray Vaughan

Following hot on the heels of "Love Struck Baby" on *Texas Flood* is "Pride and Joy." This marching boogie shuffle is the epitome of strutting Texas blues, part low-down Lightnin' Hopkins, part flashy Freddie King, and all Stevie Ray Vaughan machismo.

While maintaining the energy and excitement of "Love Struck Baby," albeit at a more relaxed and swinging tempo, "Pride and Joy" is the first studio evidence of one of Stevie's greatest strengths. Besides being a shockingly fast and facile lead player, he was an exemplary trio guitarist, blending lead lines, chords, fills, and embellishments with consummate skill. These attributes, along with two jackhammer solos, are presented in all their pride and joy on this guitar, bass, and drums masterpiece.

Figure 1 Study

The sixteen-measure intro of "Pride and Joy" serves as a blueprint for the regular twelve-bar verses which follow in giddy succession. Being in the country bluesman's key of E, open strings are allowed to ring like bells in the four-measure unaccompanied section. Derived from three boxes of the E blues scale the implied harmony is E (I chord) major. Stevie Ray's rock solid sense of time is evident in the way his swinging eighth notes walk right into the instrumental verse and join up with the bass and drums.

The twelve-bar section of the intro pumps along in the manner of boogie woogie piano. Stevie Ray's rhythmic vision is so sharp that the combination of walking bass lines and chords sound like two guitarists. On top of that, his rhythm guitar playing is as compelling as his soloing!

Figure 1 Performance

Measure 1 matches the root (E), fretted, with the droning, open high E string as a unison, not unlike the first notes of "Hey Joe." In measure 2, Stevie Ray calls up a familiar, country blues train whistle by bending the flatted 3rd (G) of E up a quarter step, *almost* to the major 3rd (G♯). At the same time, he picks the 5th (B), *almost* creating a dyad of a 3rd. It is close enough for blues, to be sure, identifying the underlying harmony as continuing in E. Measure 3 returns to fret 5 with the unison E notes of measure 1. Measure 4 caps the sequence with a swoop down to the open position box of the E blues scale and a half-step bend to the ♭5th that resolves to the root. As a portent of things to come, he inserts open strings on the "and," or off beat, of beats 1 and 4. The open A, D, and G strings, while upstanding citizens of the E blues scale, add a bluesy dissonance for effect, rather than actually reinforcing the chord change. The open G, B, and E strings however, suggest the I chord while acting as a "pick up" into measure 5 (the 12 bar section).

Now the goodies: The four measures of the I chord intertwine the root, 3rd, 5th, and 6th as walking bass notes from the E Mixolydian mode with the open G, B, and E strings (except for beat 1 of measure 7 which contains the G♯ (3rd) instead of the G, forming an E/G♯ inverted triad). An E major tonality is implied, even with that ♭3rd "blue note!" Please be aware of pick stroke direction (strict down and up) as indicated above the staff. Also, check out the ♭3rd as a hammer-on to the major 3rd on beat 2 of each measure; be sure to sustain the 3rd as you up-stroke on the open strings. In addition, note the chordal embellishment on beat 4 of measure 6. Stevie Ray smacks the A, C♯, and F♯ notes on the top three strings, suggesting an A6 (or quick I-IV move) that resolves back to a complete E triad.

Measure 9—moving to the IV (A) chord—maintains the same open strings while changing the bass line to the relative notes of the A Mixolydian mode. The open strings now imply the ♭7th (G), 9th (B) and 5th (E) of A. In measure 6 Stevie Ray throws in the A6-E from measure 5.

Measures 11 and 12 mainly repeat measures 5 and 6 except for the triplet on beat 4 of measure 12. The implied B6 tonality of the resulting double-stop leads into the V (B) chord change in measure 13 with élan. Here Stevie deviates from the bass/chord thump of the preceding eight measures and dips back into the E blues scale in the open position. By repeating the B6 dyad and B note itself, he establishes the V chord with a high degree of certainty. In measure 14 (back on the IV chord) he continues his slalom down the E blues scale, this time bumping the A notes along the way.

Measure 15 resolves back to the I chord with the top three open strings and the D/B dyad from measures 12 and 13. With the change to E, the dyad transforms into the 5th and ♭7th, a favorite lick of both Lightnin' Hopkins and John Lee Hooker. Measure 16 uses the bass notes from the E blues scale to walk from the root to the 5th.

Figure 1

* Chord symbols represent overall harmony.

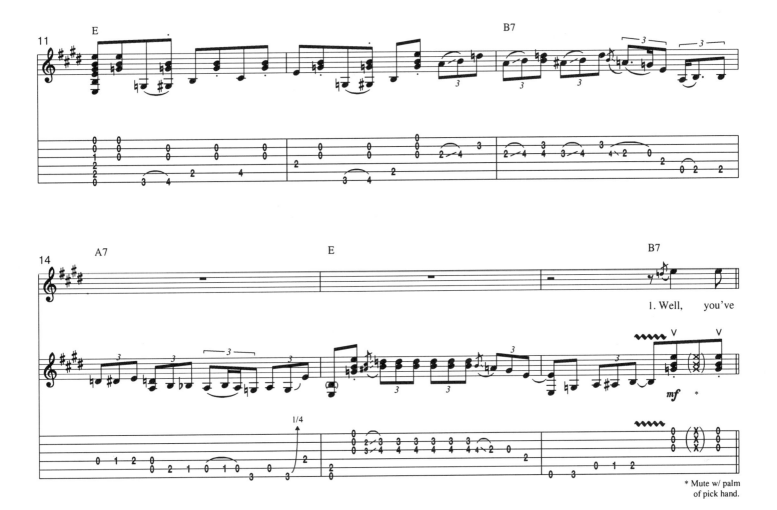

Figure 2 Study

The first solo from "Pride and Joy" exhibits another one of Stevie Ray Vaughan's many virtues—his tasty and judicious use of theme and variation. Along with the structural placement of chord tones and embellishments, themes and their variations promote continuity and can act as "hooks" to grab the listener's attention.

Each twelve-bar chorus of this twenty-four-measure solo contains licks and variations first seen in the intro. Foremost among these is the insistent whine of the high E string, coupled with movable double-stops. Additionally, bass notes and open bass strings contribute contrapuntal dynamics, welcome low end frequencies, and chord identification as they did previously.

Figure 2 Performance

In measures 1 and 2, an E/G♯ major triad at fret 12 is proffered, similar to the "Dust My Broom" slide guitar lick nurtured by Elmore James. However, rather than barring across the three top strings, Mr. SRV plays the root E note open. The lowered octave adds fullness, while recalling the drone sound played in the intro. In measure 3 the dyad on the G and B strings is moved up to fret 15, implying a change from an E major to an E7 chord. Measure 4 is the same as measure 2.

Chuck Berry's "Johnny B. Goode" lick with the bent G string (measure 5) breaks from the chordal triplets of the first three measures. Though this phrase tends to function most efficiently over the I chord, it is repeated, with slight variation, over the IV chord in measure 6. (Note: Mr. Berry does the same thing in JBG, except that he *starts* the lick on the IV chord, continuing with it as a tension and release device). Inasmuch as the B♭, B, and E notes now are operating as the ♭9th, 9th, and 5th of A, they *do* harmonize. They are not as "inside" though, as would occur if the entire lick was moved up to fret 17 of the A blues box.

Be that as it may, Stevie Ray boils the lick down to a series of quarter- and full-step bends on the G string at fret 14 in measure 7. The effect is one of anticipation of the upcoming I chord in measure 8, with the B note functioning as the 5th of E, wanting to resolve to the root. Indeed it does, on the last beat of measure 7, as well as three times in measure 8. In measure 9, a large intervallic leap of register (and faith!) is made, as Stevie Ray glisses twelve big frets down to fret 2 on the G string, thereby landing back home in the open position of the E blues scale. A walk from the I to the V chord finds the V7 (B7) chord being picked apart while measure 11 nails the IV chord with a swooping octave gliss from fret 5, to fret 17, and back. A wicked double-stop "smear" of the G/D notes at fret 3, along with a double-stop containing a ♭9th (B♭) and a fourth (D) that *somehow* manages to reach the root (A) of the IV chord in measure 11 before slamming back to the I chord in measure 12. Again, the D/B dyad in the open position is harnessed to imply an E7 chord. Measure 13 closes out the first chorus with a jazzy ♯V9-V9 chordal hit, then winds back into that unison "E lick" as a pick up into the next twelve-bar chorus.

Measure 14 charges off like the intro with the unison "E lick" followed by the "train whistle" bend in measure 15. The next two measures continue this alternating sequence with the IV chord change in measures 18 and 19, implying an A7 chord by using the 5th (E) and ♭7th (G) notes shimmering with the open, high E string. Check the time warping, *quarter-note* triplets in measures 17 and 18 before you go any further. It has been said that Clapton, in his Bluesbreakers days, could make "time stand still" on a good night, here Stevie Ray easily pulls it off with the aural evidence to back it up.

Measures 20 and 21 find SRV back down in the open position of the E blues scale once again, as he brings this bucking bronco of a solo back to the paddock. As usual, roots, ♭7ths, and 5ths abound, with the strong "target note" of a major 3rd (G♯) snuck in for good measure! Measure 22 has virtually the same broken B7 arpeggio as measure 10. The IV chord in measure 23 is given a glancing acknowledgment with 4ths, 9ths, and a couple of roots, as Stevie Ray speeds through on the way to his resolution on the I chord in measure 24. Likewise, almost a carbon copy of measure 12, measure 24 cruises in with a bass note walk to the 5th, followed by the open G, B, and E strings, as yet another pick up into the next verse.

Figure 2

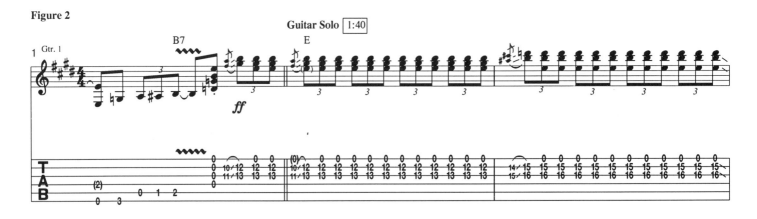

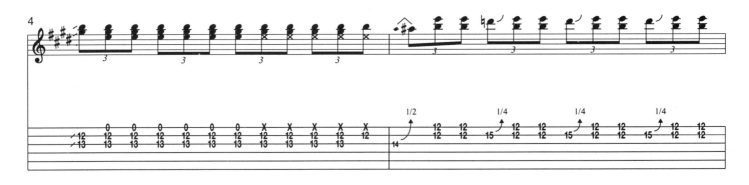

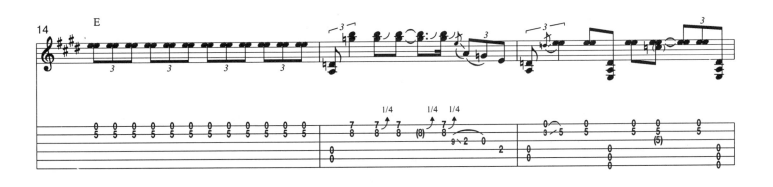

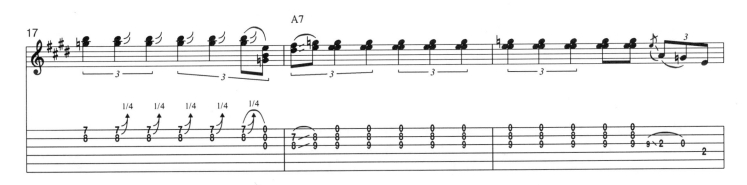

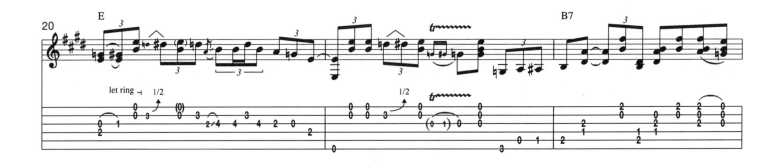

Figure 3 Study

The twelve-bar outro keeps all the balls in the air by restating the main themes of the intro and solos. Triplet double-stops at several positions, plus some soaring bends above fret 12 for "seasoning," wrap up this guitar cornucopia.

Figure 3 Performance

Measures 1-4 motor up the fingerboard with four implied inversions of E chords. Measure 1 suggests E7/B with a double-stop of D/B, transforming to a three-note chord with the addition of the open high E string. In this context, measure 2 functions as an E6/C♯ with the C♯ and fretted E notes, and the open high E string (Note: If the indicated chord was A (IV), the implied harmony would be an A/C♯ inverted triad). The G♯, B, and open, high E notes in measure 3 combine to form an E/G♯ triad, while measure 4 is the same as measure 1, one octave higher.

In measure 5, Stevie Ray manhandles a group of notes relating to A7, A6, and A9 at the 12th position. Guitar Slim (Eddie Jones), one of his more obscure idols, often played similar combinations, most notably in "The Things I Used to Do." Of course, Slim probably never bent that A6 triple-stop in *quite* the same way, but then again, no one ever played like Stevie Ray—then or now.

Measure 6 starts a five measure cascade of bent and tortured notes, all pulled from the E blues scale in its root position at fret 12. To be honest, Stevie Ray is letting go here, not paying absolute attention to note selection as the chords change. That said, his innate sense of logic compels him to repeatedly bend up to the root (A) of the IV chord in measure 6 and to bang on the roots and 5ths of the I chord in measures 7 and 8. In measure 9, over the V chord (the critical juncture of any 12 bar blues), he hammers an F♯ (5th) along with the root B. He follows that in measure 10 (the IV chord) with double-stops and bends relating to A9 and sus7 chords.

As at the end of each twelve-bar verse, Stevie Ray drops back to the open position of E for the last two turnaround measures. With ♭3rds, and even a major 7 note flying around in measure 11, he correctly resolves the tension by landing on the G♯ (3rd) target note before finding his way to the penultimate B9 which leads to the final chord, a prickly E7♯9.

Figure 3

Outro Guitar Solo 3:10

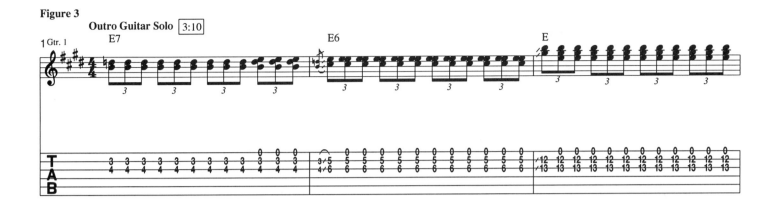

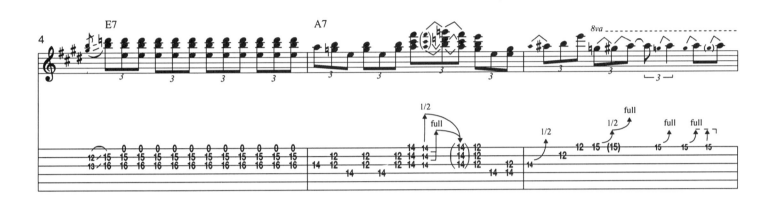

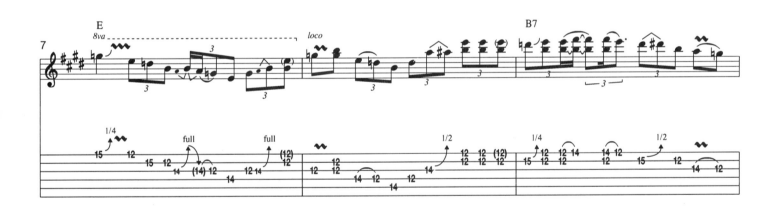

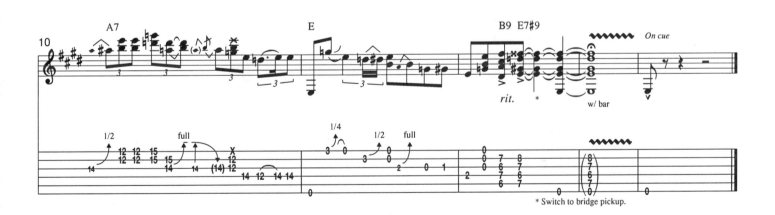

* Switch to bridge pickup.

RUDE MOOD
(Texas Flood)
Written by Stevie Ray Vaughan

Cocky rock and blues guitarists who were smugly listening their way through the selections on *Texas Flood* had to be brought up short by "Rude Mood." A delusional wiseacre could *possibly* dismiss the mid-tempo rockers, shuffles, and slow blues on side 1 as the work of a skilled and knowledgeable technical craftsman. But no one, with perhaps the exception of Danny Gatton, could have helped being blasted back to reality by the warp speed of "Rude Mood."

Pale by comparison, antecedents for this type of boogie shuffle can be found in rockabilly and the country "jazzabilly" of Jimmy Bryant and Speedy West in the fifties. Arthur Smith's "Guitar Boogie Shuffle," re-recorded by the Virtues in 1959, was built around a prominent boogie bass line, as was "Hot Rod Lincoln" by Commander Cody in the early seventies. Most significantly, blues legend Lightnin' Hopkins scorched his way through an amazing group of electric boogie tunes for the Herald record label in Houston, in 1954.

The down side of Stevie Ray's pyrotechnical barrage on "Rude Mood" was the moronic title of "the world's fastest guitarist" bestowed on him by some misguided promo person. It was like being called "the fastest gun in the West"—it meant that a reputation was on the line every time he played. No doubt the stress from this kind of pressure contributed to his burnout in the late eighties. It is a credit to the man, and his music, that he was able to overcome the reputation and its resulting addiction.

Figure 1 Study

Except for letter T, where Stevie plays a twenty-six-measure chorus consisting of four measures of E (I), twenty measures of A (IV), and two measures of ♭ (V), "Rude Mood" is a lengthy series of twelve-bar blues choruses.

The intro (letter A) lays out the basic boogie bass line as the underlying structure of the piece.

Figure 1 Performance

(WARNING! You should know that the speed and swinging nature of "Rude Mood" requires almost total down and up pick strokes)

Though not as dynamic as "Pride and Joy" in its mix of walking bass lines and chordal stabs, a similar effect is produced on the I and IV chords.

By anchoring your index finger with a small barre on the A and D strings at fret 2, you will be able to hit the double stop, and reach the bass notes, without changing your hand position for the I chord in measures 1-4 and 7 and 8. By shifting over one string so that you are covering the D and G strings, you can play the same relative pattern for the IV chord in measures 5 and 6. Notice that the first twelve-bar chorus infers a iim chord in measure 9 where you would normally expect to find the V7 chord. The iim, or *its* substitute, the II7, is a common substitution for the V chord in blues, R&B, and jazz.

Do not overlook the fact that the bass line connecting measures 9 and 10 is *almost* the same ascending as descending. The A♯ notes on beat four of measure 9 are left out on the way down in measure 10, as they would infer a non-bluesy major 7th in relationship to the B chord change; in respect to the F♯m chord in measure 9, the A♯ is the ♭3rd.

Figure 1

Tune Down 1/2 Step:
①= Eb ④= Db
②= Bb ⑤= Ab
③= Gb ⑥= Eb

A Intro
Fast Shuffle ♩ = 264
Gtr. 1 (band tacet) N.C.(E)

Figure 2 Study

Part B is a twelve-bar solo guitar chorus, sans bass and drums. This tour de force bristles with punctual eighth notes marking the passage of time as surely as any rhythm section.

Two of Stevie Ray's Texas predecessors, Clarence "Gatemouth" Brown and Eddie "Guitar Slim" Jones, played boogies similarly (if slower!) to the one at letter B. Check out Gate's "Atomic Energy," "Boogie Uproar," and "Gate Walks to Board." Slim's "Guitar Slim Boogie" and "Guitar Slim" should prove to be equally illuminating.

Figure 2 Performance

Use alternate down and up pick strokes, play as fast as you can, and hold on to your butt! But seriously folks, this is more about clean articulation and steady, swinging meter than it is about careful note selection. Nonetheless, measures 5 and 6 (over the IV (A) chord) do contain some extremely juicy major 2nds (B) and 3rds (C♯). The rest is merely rapid pentatonic studies in the root position of the E blues scale at fret 12 and in the open string position.

Make sure you scan measure 10 where Stevie Ray modulates to the ♯V chord and back to the V—yet another way of dealing with measures 9 and 10 in terms of substitutions.

Figure 2

Figure 3 Study

Reaching deep into his bag of tricks at letter G, Stevie Ray hauls out a series of dynamic octaves in a pattern vaguely reminiscent of the stop-time break in "Hideaway."

Figure 3 Performance

Though it sounds like he is using his flatpick to jump from the bass to the treble side, a hybrid combination of pick and finger works splendidly. Try it like this: with the pick held in the normal position between the thumb and index finger, reach with the middle finger to pluck the high E (and B in measure 4) string.

The descending pattern in measures 3 and 4 consists of the root, 6th, #5th, 5th, 3rd, ♭3rd, 2nd, and root (an octave lower). You could address this sequence of notes as the major scale (Ionian mode) jazzed up with the #5th and ♭3rd as cool passing tones.

Figure 3

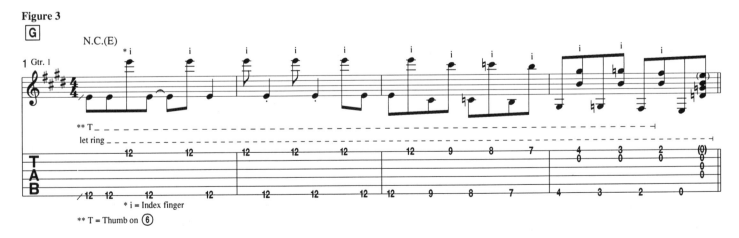

Figure 4 Study

Casting aside all pretense, Stevie Ray quotes almost verbatim from the breakdown in "Hideaway" at letter K. Additionally, the A7 chord in measure 6 is a preview of the driving chordal choruses that follow later and bring the tune to a smashing climax.

Figure 4 Performance

Here is the fingering for the E9/D inversion in measures 1-3: ring finger = string 4, middle finger = string 3, index finger = string 2, pinky = string 1.

As notated between the staff and tablature in measures 3 and 4, use the hybrid picking technique described in the performance notes of Figure 3 for the double stops.

Stevie Ray struts his mastery of texture and dynamics in measures 5-8. The A boogie line in measure 5 sets up the open A7 chord in measure 6, as the E boogie line in measure 7 walks up to the implied E major chord in measure 8.

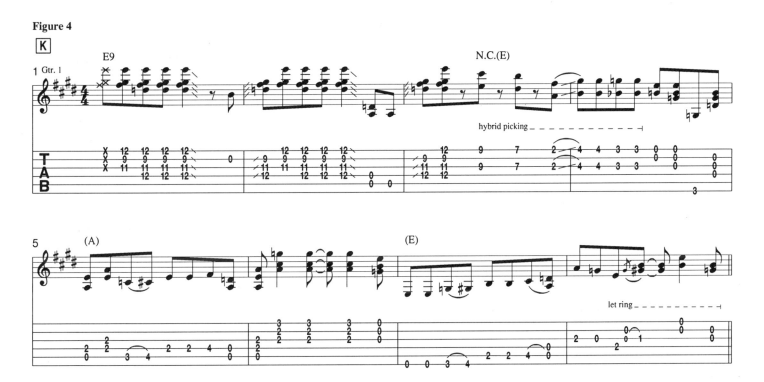

Figure 4

Figure 5 Study

Letter L has a heart-stopping bass line in measures 1-10 that brings to mind "Stratosphere Boogie" (1953) by Jimmy Bryant and Speedy West. The bass line is a two measure phrase that ascends in the first measure and descends in the second. The whole chorus is comprised of eighth notes save for two measly rests. At 264 bpm it is a sweat-popping workout for both hands.

Along with letter S, letter L has the most single notes and the fewest double stops and chords in "Rude Mood."

Figure 5 Performance

The bass notes traverse their respective scales like an Olympic skier schussing over moguls. As has been the case throughout these lessons, rapid and accurate down and up pick strokes are a strict requirement for the faithful execution of the piece.

Besides the two-measure increments, letter L has a sub-structure. The open B and high E strings that sustain across the bar line of measures 3 and 4, and the same open strings in measure 8, give the impression that a four-measure phrase is also being demarcated. In other words, the effect is one of the bass line rushing head long towards the upper strings, culminating in a double or triple stop. Though it may be subtle in contrast to the six string fireworks going off all around it, the musical expressiveness of this section only adds to the exhilaration of this rocket ride.

Figure 5

Figure 6 Study

The simplicity of lettert S is a welcome respite from the rush of notes that precedes it. Stevie mutes and snaps strings in a blues technique that stretches back at least as far as Delta blues pioneer Charlie Patton (the beginning of the 20th century). Except for the turnaround in measures 11 and 12, an especially sparse arrangement of notes is used to signal the chord changes.

Figure 6 Performance

SRV uses the major 3rd (G#) target note to proclaim measures 1-4 as being in the key of E major. However, he surprises us in measures 5 and 6 with the 9th of A (IV) where we might expect the more common root, 3rd, or 5th. Measure 7 uses the open high E (root) while measure 8 has the 2nd (F#) and 3rd (G#).

Another surprise awaits in measures 9 and 10 where he plays the 5th (B) and 4th (A) notes, implying a V-IV chord change where iim-V and V-#V-V changes had occurred in earlier choruses. These are the more standard chord changes in measures 9 and 10 of a 12-bar blues.

Figure 6

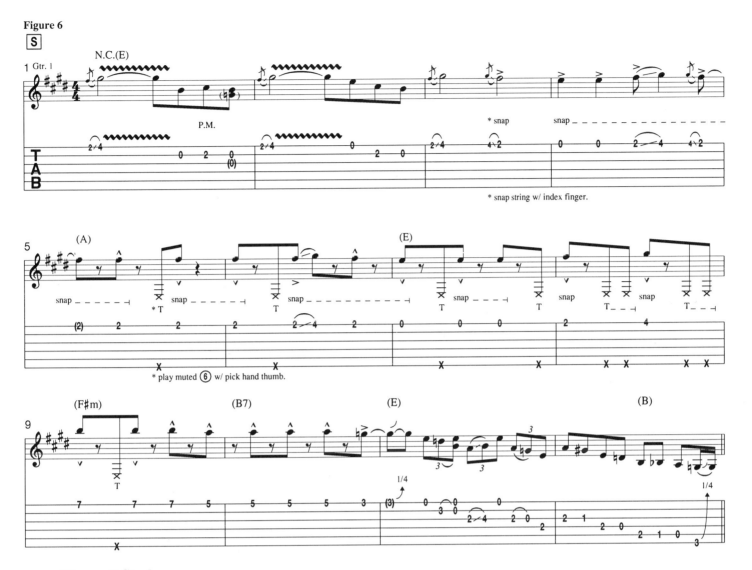

* snap string w/ index finger.

* play muted ⑥ w/ pick hand thumb.

Figure 7 Study

Letter T kicks the hell out of the twelve-bar pattern our ears have become so accustomed to expecting. After making the usual change to the IV (A) chord in measure 5, the progression stays on the IV chord for the next *sixteen* measures. You do not pass go, collect $200, or return to the I chord, but instead rock right to the V chord in measures 25 and 26!

Stevie builds up a terrific head of steam by starting with open position E blues scale licks and climaxing with upper register A9 chords. In between, he plays some pedestrian A7 voicings in the lower register as a transition.

You should know that a similar chordal idea, in a much more condensed form (of course), is presented in Lonnie Mack's "Wham" from 1963.

Figure 7 Performance

Technically, there is nothing tricky about this extended chorus. It is the concept of building tension and excitement through repetition that is paramount to the lesson.

The ease with which you grab the Freddie King 9th chord inversion in measures 19-24 will be somewhat dictated by the type of guitar you play. A Strat, like Stevie brandished, has a narrow enough neck and is cut away sufficiently to allow clear access to the upper frets. A Les Paul, by contrast, with its thicker neck joint, might have you pulling your thumb back from the edge of the fingerboard and pointing in a direction *parallel* to the length of the neck towards the headstock.

Figure 7

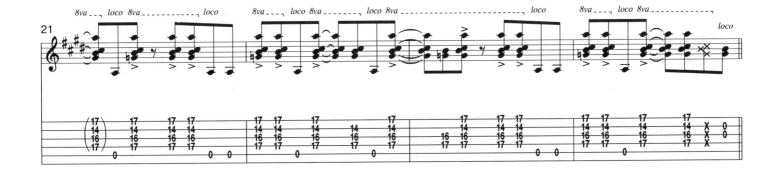

Figure 8 Study

Letter V reiterates the chordal barrage of letter T with the same 9th chord inversion over the I chord change. A standard blues 9th chord voicing is used for the IV and V chord changes.

Be aware at letter U, Stevie Ray inserted a chorus of open string boogie licks as a dynamic contrast between the high register, dense chordal choruses of letters T and V.

Figure 8 Performance

Except for a handful of intuitively placed eighth-note rests, letter V is crammed with eighth-note chords. As this is mainly a lesson in right hand control, you should experiment with various patterns of down and up strokes. Stevie Ray *tends* to use mostly down strokes, except on beat three of measures 1, 2, 3, 4, 5, 7, and 9, where he slaps in an up stroke to swing the second eighth note.

Ever the master of rhythm, as well as lead, Stevie Ray was one of the few blues guitarists to make chords such an important part of his approach to soloing. Lonnie Mack with his "Wham," "Down and Out," and the bluesy version of Chuck Berry's "Memphis" (all from 1963) employed chords in the heads or solos. Freddie King with "Hideaway" (1961) and "In the Open" (1962) also qualifies as a member of this exclusive club. Inquiring minds will want to know Lonnie and Freddie recorded in Cincinnati for Fraternity and King records in the early sixties. More to the point, it is reported Lonnie played on some of Freddie's tracks. He was also a session guitarist for King records around the same time.

Figure 8

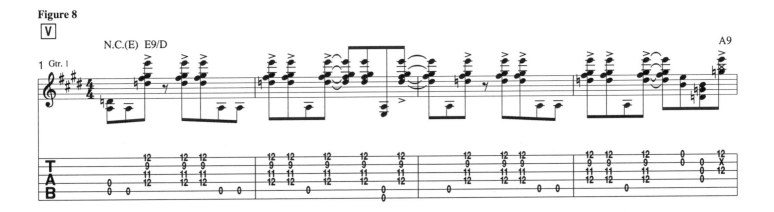

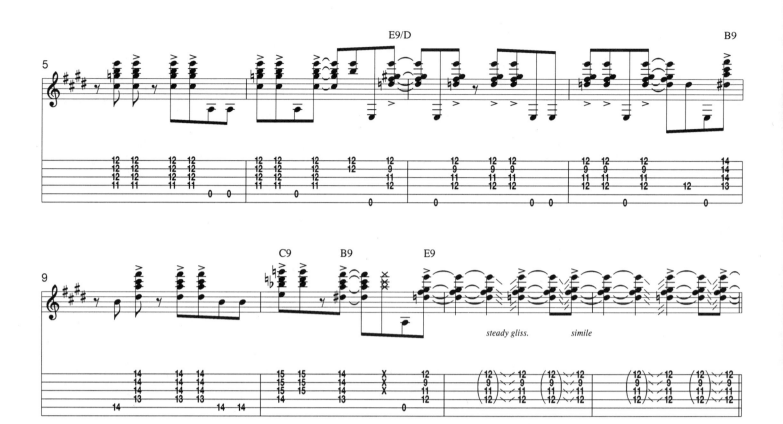

LENNY
(Texas Flood)
Written by Stevie Ray Vaughan

As the closing curtain on *Texas Flood*, "Lenny" is a lovely instrumental ballad in the manner of "Have You Ever Been (To Electric Ladyland)" and "Moon, Turn the Tides.....Gently, Gently Away" by Jimi Hendrix from his *Electric Ladyland* album (1968). A great deal of this tune's seductiveness comes from the "out of phase" Strat tone, produced by placing the pick-up selector switch in the notch between the neck and middle pick ups. Jimi's "The Wind Cries Mary" is also a superb example of this rich, warm sound.

"Lenny" intros and outros with freely phrased I-IV vamps of seven measures. Letters B and D (the head) are eight measures in length with a pattern of I, IV, I, IV, V, II, ♭III and IV. Letter C is sixteen alternating measures of I and IV. Letter E contains twenty-four measures of the same.

Stevie Ray honored his wife Lenny with this beautiful composition.

Figure 1 Study

The head (letters B and D) is an exemplary introductory lesson in the chord melody style of Mr. Jimi Hendrix. Bass notes, four and five string chords, plus triple and double stops mesh with scalar passages to delineate the inferred chord changes.

Figure 1 Performance

Measure 1 begins with a typical Hendrixism. The root bass note is struck, followed by an Emaj13 chord and an E Mixolydian mode fragment containing the root, 2nd (or 9th), 3rd, and 5th. Measure 2 continues this pattern over the IV chord with the root (A), triple-stop chords (A7-A6) and a run up the A major (Ionian) scale. Measure 3 sandwiches the Emaj13 chord between a common double stop of a fourth and the same lick as in measure 1. A sequence inferring A, A6, B6, and B♭6 chords follows in measure 4, with sliding triple stops and the root, 3rd, and 5th from a B♭ arpeggio moving to a B6 arpeggiation in measure 5.

Measures 6 and 7 continue with the same fingering pattern and technique begun in measure 5. The thumb is hooked over the edge of the fingerboard to catch the bass notes while the 3rd, 5th, and 6th of the D and G major scales infer a D6 (measure 6) and a G6 (measure 7).

Measure 8 implies a B♭6 with a root, 3rd, 5th, and 6th arpeggio, followed by an A6 chord and a pick-up lick from the E Aeolian (natural minor) mode leading to the E chord inferred in measure 1 of letter C. Since there are no chords under the melody, and the bass is only playing the root (E) note on the down beat of measure 1 in letter C, major *or* minor scales can be discreetly interchanged.

Figure 1

Figure 2 Study

The twenty-four measures of letter E form the longest improvised section of "Lenny." As we drift through the I-IV chord changes, Stevie Ray takes us on a musical journey in the company of his two main idols, Jimi Hendrix and Albert King. As I-IV chord changes are at the heart of blues, R&B, and rock, knowledge of the numerous ways they can be negotiated is paramount to achieving musical excellence.

Figure 2 Performance

Because this entire section is composed of I (E) and IV (A) chord changes lasting one measure each, it would behoove us to analyze them accordingly.

The I chords break down as such:

<u>Measure 1</u> = The low E string and that old, familiar E/B double stop.

Measure 3 = Starting with the root at fret 7, string 5, Stevie Ray hammers and pulls his way through the root position of the C♯ blues scale between frets 9 and 12. The C♯ scale functions as the relative minor to E major. This user friendly blues scale contains the melodic major 3rd, 2nd (9th), 5th, and 6th notes from the E major (Ionian) scale. Tossed in for blues appeal is the ♭3rd (G), which would be the ♭5th of the C♯ scale if we were in the key of C♯.

Measure 5 = Paydirt! These types of double stops were used by Hendrix in "The Wind Cries Mary" and "Hey Joe." The combination of the root (E) with the 6th (C♯), 3rd (G♯), 5th (B), and 2nd (F♯) provides a wonderful array of major scale harmonies.

Measure 7 = A descending E blues scale run that starts with a half-step bend of G (♭3rd), to G♯ (major 3rd, leading tone), and resolves to the root.

Measure 9 = A dynamic dip down to the open position and the bass strings, courtesy of the E Mixolydian mode. Adding to the dynamics is the sense of space engendered by the rest at the beginning of the measure. Measures 9-13, of both the I and IV chords, are in this vein. Note the change of guitar tone from the funky out of phase position, to the clanky bridge pick-up for that classic blues tone.

Measure 11 = For a guitarist who was wont to use ten notes where two would suffice, Stevie Ray relies almost entirely on the root (E), and ♭7th (D) to carry the day. Of course they are phrased in sixteenth- note triplets, but at a leisurely 62 bpm this sounds as relaxed as a walk in the park! In beat 3 the emphasis shifts to the A, E, and G notes, setting up the IV chord in measure 12 with the root, 5th, and ♭7th of A.

Measure 13 = Stevie Ray plucks the major 3rd (G♯), and the 4th (A) from the E Mixolydian mode. Again, simplicity rules the day and it is a benign despot.

Measure 15 = Stevie zooms to the upper register with some blues scale noodling at fret 12. Pretty standard fare except for the sustained and vibratoed ♭3rd adding a bit of pungent bluesiness to the generally melodic proceedings of the piece.

Measure 17 = Albert King redux! E blues scale quarter-, half- and full-step bends abound above fret 12. The A (4th) to B (5th) string squeezers at fret 17 are, along with the same bends in measure 19, literally the *high* point of the song.

Measure 19 = More high altitude riffing in the "Albert King box," an octave above where the "V-Master" would normally play it.

Measure 21 = Bass string E Mixolydian mode bashing around fret 12. The inclusion of the *open* low E string, vibratoed with the whammy bar, is a dynamic release from the previous musical tension.

Measure 23 = Chiming E, D, and G harmonics from the E blues scale; short and sweet.

And ... now for the IV chord investigation:

Measure 2 = Stevie Ray locks his thumb over the neck at fret 5 so that he can arpeggiate the 3rd and 5th notes with the A (root). He then slips into the little A major scale box at fret 7 that is tucked behind
the root position of the A major and blues scales at fret 5. Hendrix used this system for applying melodic fills in all of his chord melody work.

Measure 4 = Similar to beats 3 and 4 of measure 2. Between frets 7 and 11 on strings E (6), A, and D, the 2nd, 3rd, 5th, and 6th notes from the A major scale lie in close proximity to each other in a *blues* scale-type fingering. Think pentatonic licks and you end up with melodic, major scale tones. It should all be this easy!!

Measure 6 = Continues the theme of measures 2 and 4, while incorporating a cool double-stop hammer-on lick (a la Jimi) containing the 3rd and 5th.

Measure 8 = The E blues scale at fret 12 with the B/G and C♯/A double stops emphasized to infer the ♭7th (G), 9th (B), 3rd (C♯), and root notes of the A Mixolydian mode.

Measure 10 = Moving up to the second position (from the open position in measure 9), Stevie Ray transforms the E major scale into the A Mixolydian mode by including the G (♭7th of A) bent up a full step to the root (A).

Measure 12 = Continues with a similar pattern as was started in measure 11 of the I chord. A sextuplet consisting of the ♭2nd, root, and ♭7th (in the key of A) is repeated, moving to the root and ♭7th on beats 3 and 4.

Measure 14 = The second position A major chord is used as a broken arpeggio, followed by an open string trill of E (5th) to D (4th) in beats 1 and 2. As he does throughout "Lenny," Stevie Ray commandeers the last two beats of the measure as a pick-up into the next. In measure 14, he accomplishes this by implying a switch to the E blues scale with the E (root), D (♭7th), a G/D open string double stop (implying the ♭7th and bluesy ♭3rd) then flying up to the E blues box at fret 12 for a quarter step bend of the A (4th), released to a sustained, vibratoed G (♭3rd).

Measure 16 = (see measure 15)

Measure 18 = Similar to measure 17, with extra focus on the ♭7th (G) of A.

Measure 20 = Yeow! Rampant single string and double-stop bends between frets 12 and 15 of the E blues scale. *Mucho* emphasis on the ♭7th (G), 9th (B), root (A), 3rd (C♯), and 5th (E) of the A Mixolydian mode. Beaucoup thirty-second notes in quintuplets and sextuplets blur together to give an *aural* impression of an A dominant tonality.

Measure 22 = Whew! A welcome respite from the compressed tension of the previous measures, as Stevie Ray simply and gracefully arpeggiates an A6 chord at fret 5.

Measure 24 = A raked and strummed A6 chord, with the C♯ minor scale (relative to E) at fret 9 explored as a pick-up into letter F on beats 3 and 4.

Figure 2

28

COULDN'T STAND THE WEATHER
Epic Records 39304 (1984)

Brimming with confidence from the stunning critical response to *Texas Flood*, Stevie Ray Vaughan took the music wider and deeper into his roots with *Couldn't Stand the Weather*. Compared to the hurried "demo" conditions under which the first album was recorded, this time the band had a relatively leisurely three weeks in New York with John Hammond supervising. Brother Jimmie took time off from playing guitar with the Fabulous Thunderbirds to play on the title track and "The Things I Used to Do," as did T-Birds drummer Fran Christina on "Stang's Swang." The eight selections ranging from slow blues to funk, rock, and jazz, were evenly divided between sharp originals and cool covers.

Picking up where "Rude Mood" left off, "Scuttle Buttin'" is a fast, instrumental rock shuffle with a knuckle-numbing head. The title tune is a prime cut of soulful funk that would not have been out of place on *The Band of Gypsys*. Stevie Ray tipped his cowboy hat towards the legendary Guitar Slim with his steaming take on "The Things I Used to Do." After hinting at Hendrix on "Lenny" from *Texas Flood*, he did a startlingly accurate version of Jimi's "Voodoo Chile (Slight Return)."

Side two of the disc boogies with the hip R&B of Mike Kindred's "Cold Shot," followed by a long, moody, and dramatic reading of the slow minor blues classic "Tin Pan Alley." Stevie's mid-tempo shuffle "Honey Bee" then sets up the swinging jazz on display in "Stang's Swang."

Carefully hand picked for your musical edification are "Scuttle Buttin'," "Couldn't Stand the Weather," "Cold Shot," and "Stang's Swang."

SCUTTLE BUTTIN'
(Couldn't Stand the Weather)
Written by Stevie Ray Vaughan

Stevie Ray threw down the gauntlet to guitarists of all stripes with the head to "Scuttle Buttin'." While owing a debt to Lonnie Mack's "Wham," the profusion of sixteenth notes played at 160 bpm puts this number in a class of its own. Fortunately it is only 1:49 in length.

Figure 1 Study

The twelve-bar head is constructed around a slashing, one measure open position E blues scale run which precedes the I, IV, and V chord changes. This lick is almost exactly the same each time it is rendered, ending on the root note of the chord change.

In a way that is consistent with one aspect of Stevie's rhythm guitar style, the chords are implied by root bass notes and double stops.

Figure 1 Performance

The demonic speed required to play the head makes alternate down and up pick strokes absolutely necessary. Starting with the pick up, try ↓,↓,↑,↓,↑ (slide/hammer), ↓,↓,↑ (pull-off), ↓ (bend, release, pull-off), ↑, and ↓ for the root note.

By the way, the drone of the open strings, particularly the high E, gives the impression the lick is even faster than it is as it blurs by.

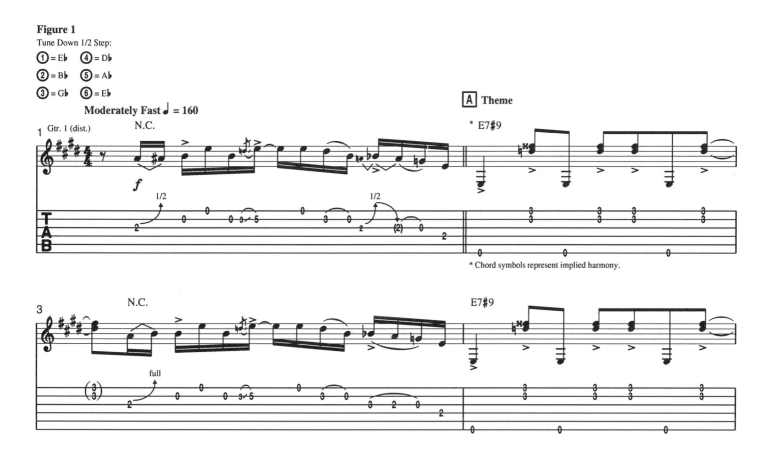

Figure 1
Tune Down 1/2 Step:
① = E♭   ④ = D♭
② = B♭   ⑤ = A♭
③ = G♭   ⑥ = E♭

Moderately Fast ♩ = 160

Gtr. 1 (dist.)   N.C.   [A] Theme   * E7♯9

* Chord symbols represent implied harmony.

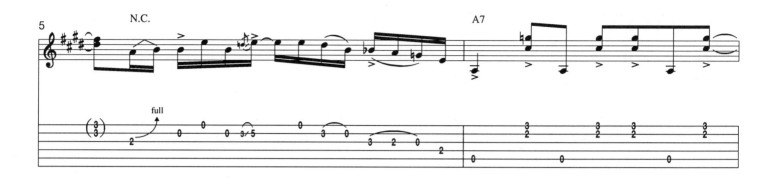

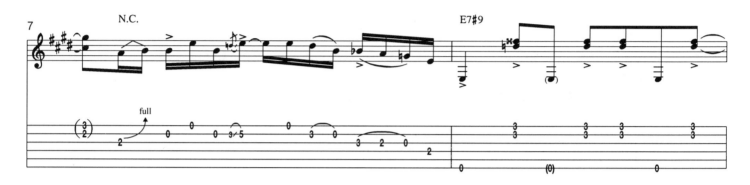

Figure 2 Study

The twelve-bar solo chorus of letter D spotlights Stevie Ray's creative and logical use of double stops. Only measures 2, 9, and 10 are predominately scalar.

Figure 2 Performance

Measure 1 cavalierly enlists the bent G-string lick from the head by moving it an octave up the neck. The double stop of a fourth (E/B) has been used by everyone from Robert Johnson to Chuck Berry to identify chord (E major) changes. Measure 2 continues the theme established in measure 1, adding typical G-string bends along with pulls and hammers (involving the ♭3rd and root) from the 12th position of the E blues scale.

Measure 3 gets low down and greasy as Stevie Ray plays double stops that lean heavily on the blues-approved dissonant ♭3rd, rather than the consonant major 3rd against the I chord. That is okay though, because in measure 4 he alternates ♭3rd/6th dyads with 3rd/♭7th ones to tease the ear towards the E dominant tonality indicated by the chord change.

In measures 5 and 6 he really gets cute by lowering the double stops by a half step to suggest the A7 chord change. Note that the G/C♯, approached from below by a half step, is the ♭7th (leading tone) and major 3rd (target note) of A respectively.

Measures 7 and 8 of the I chord introduce a triple stop containing (low to high) D, G♯, and B implying an E7 chord. In measure 9 Stevie noodles in the E blues box at fret 12, using the root (E) as the sus4 of the V (B) chord and as *gravity* to help facilitate the eventual resolution to E in measures 11 and 12.

Measure 10 implies the IV (A7) chord with a series of hammers and pulls utilizing the A note along with the G (♭7th of A): on beat four Stevie inserts a pick-up into measure 11 by the addition of the B and E notes (the 5th and root of E).

The groovy E7♯9 chord is inferred in measure 11 with the open low E, D (♭7th) and G (♯9) notes. In measure 12 he stays with the inferred E chord change suggesting an E7, Esus6, and E major series of chords by the use of a descending sequence of double-stopped 3rds.

Figure 2

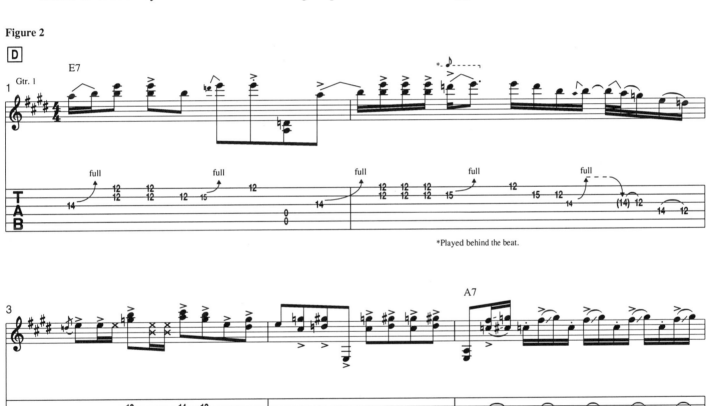

*Played behind the beat.

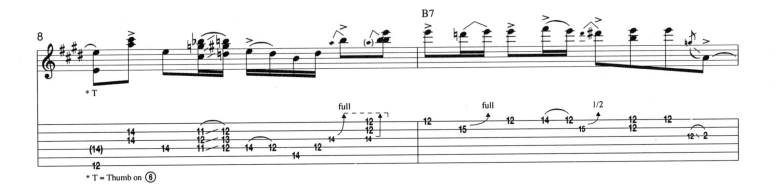

* T

* T = Thumb on ⑥

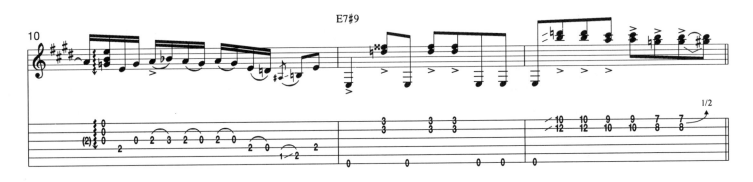

COULDN'T STAND THE WEATHER

(Couldn't Stand the Weather)

Words and Music by Stevie Ray Vaughan

Like "Lenny" from *Texas Flood*, the title track from *Couldn't Stand the Weather* shows Stevie's acknowledged debt to Jimi Hendrix. As opposed to being a dreamy ballad, though, "Couldn't Stand the Weather" is a hard funk tune that recalls Jimi's *Band of Gypsys* album.

Lyrically, Stevie spins a cautionary tale that eerily forecasts his stormy encounter with substance abuse and the dissolution of his marriage to Lenny, while fondly remembering the security of familial love. The melancholy of the minor tonalities contrasts with the energy and syncopation of the rhythms in an ominous, brooding musical statement.

Figure 1 Study

After an eight-measure intro which also serves as a vocal bridge as well as the bracketing sections of the solo, a four-measure bass-string phrase repeats two times. Plucked from the D Mixolydian mode, the root, ♭3rd (passing tone), 3rd, 4th, ♭5th (passing tone), 5th, and 7th notes are sequenced into a stuttering line that hooks itself into the memory.

Figure 1 Performance

Though technically simple to play, this phrase can be a challenge due to the syncopation of the rests and the fact they are placed differently in each measure. It would be extremely helpful to tap your foot, counting "1, 2, 3, 4" on the down beats of each measure. At the same time be aware of the up beats (when your foot is pointed up) and the notes that occur on these beats. This should help you keep track of the placement of all eighth and quarter notes.

Figure 1

The style of bass line in Figure 1 bears a strong resemblance to classic James Brown funk- like "Cold Sweat" (1967). Between the years of 1963 and 1968, the "Godfather of Soul" performed and recorded the grooviest hard funk ever heard. It has stood the test of time as the template for almost all dance music that has followed in its hypnotic wake.

Figure 2 Study

Figure 2 is another four-measure phrase, based on a two-measure increment of im-IV7 chord changes. Measures 1 and 3 are two variations of an implied Dm7, while measures 2 and 4 are two takes on an implied G dominant tonality.

Figure 2 Performance

Measure 1 starts with an F (♭3rd) octave, a double stop containing the ♭3rd (F) and 5th (A) of D, and ends with a triple-stop G6 that is bent a half step, released, and sustained across the bar line, resolving to an implied G9 in measure 2. A double stop made up of the 4th (C) and major 7th (F♯) of G adds a touch of diatonic melodicisim as Stevie Ray works over an inverted G triad (D, G, B), along with a dyad in 3rds (A/F) that implies a G9 to close measure 2.

Measure 3 uses the root, 5th, and ♭7th from the D blues scale, a *theoretical* minor scale, to casually suggest the implied Dm tonality. This is followed by a quick stab with the F♯/C dyad (from measure 2 of the IV chord) as a pick-up sustained across the bar line. Measure 4 reiterates the G triad and G9 forms seen in beats 3 and 4 of measure 2.

As you play through "Couldn't Stand the Weather," you will see that Figure 2 repeats before and after verse 1 and in the outro.

Jimi Hendrix's "Message Of Love" from his *Band of Gypsys* album has similarities to "Couldn't Stand the Weather" in its proliferation of jazzy octaves and R&B-ish I-IV chord changes.

Figure 2

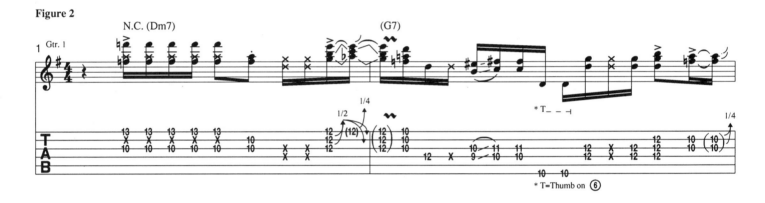

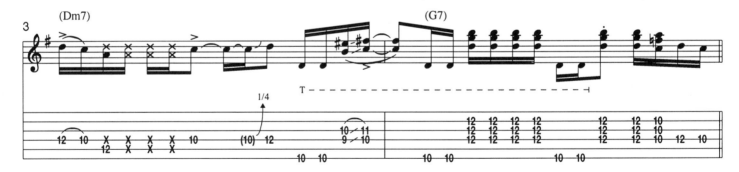

36

COLD SHOT
(Couldn't Stand the Weather)
Written by K. Kendrid

Due to its irresistibly funky shuffle beat, "Cold Shot" is probably everyone's favorite cut on *Couldn't Stand the Weather*. Though not penned by Stevie, the syncopated strums combining a simple bass figure with triads were tailor-made for his inclusive accompaniment style.

"Cold Shot" feels like a minor blues due to its im, ivm and V7 changes, even though a complete cycle (excepting the solo) consists of an eight-measure verse (im) and an *eleven* measure chorus! Because of the clever way in which the chords are arranged, we accept the odd number of measures without question. Some detective work, however, reveals the secret: two measures each of Dm7, Am7, and Dm7 for a total of six; one measure of V dominant (which feels like a natural V chord resolution after the alternating ivm-im changes); and four measures of Am7 (im). The measure of rest that precedes the chorus *feels* like it is part of the chorus, rather than the eighth measure of the verse. If we add it on to the eleven-measure chorus, voila!—12 bars of blues changes.

The leslie-like sound on Stevie Ray's guitar was achieved by running his vintage 1963 Fender Vibroverb amps through a Fender Vibratone cabinet. The rotating speaker inside the unit simulated the sound of a Hammond B-3 organ played through its companion leslie, rotating speaker enclosure. The remarkable similarity to the organ driven sound of sixties soul and R&B music completes the authentic vibe of this vibrant track.

Figure 1 Study

The eight measures of the intro also serve as the pattern for verse 1 and the coda. Though each measure is almost identical to the next, there are two different one-measure phrases at work.

The rhythm in "Cold Shot" is technically very much like "Pride and Joy" and "I'm Cryin'" from *Texas Flood*. For the most part bass notes are struck on the down beats, while chords (actual or implied) are strummed on the up beats in each measure. The effect is one of having simultaneous bass lines and chords.

Figure 1 Performance

Measures 1-3 show the basic increment for the majority of the Am7 chord changes throughout, except for the last four measures of the chorus, solo, and coda. Essentially the same pattern is employed for the Dm7 change in the chorus, albeit in the key of D at fret 10. The root (A) and ♭7th (G) notes are alternated with the muted open D, G, and B strings for three beats. On the fourth beat, inferred Bm/D and Am/C triads are strummed. (Note: these chords represent the harmonized first two degrees of either the A Aeolian or Dorian modes).

Measures 4-8 contain a variation on this pattern. The Am/C triad is sustained across the bar line from measure 3 to 4 and held for the duration of a quarter note. The chord now takes the place of the A bass note that would normally appear on the down beat of beat 1. Stevie Ray re-introduces this second pattern at the end of the chorus, and in the coda where it is repeated until the change to the E7♯9 chord.

As a quick review in muting techniques, use the index finger on your left hand to muffle the open strings. Keep the palm of your right hand close to the bridge of your guitar in order to quickly dampen the strings after you pick the bass notes. This will help to insure a suitably crisp and cold staccato attack.

Figure 1

Tune Down 1/2 Step:

① = E♭ ④ = D♭

② = B♭ ⑤ = A♭

③ = G♭ ⑥ = E♭

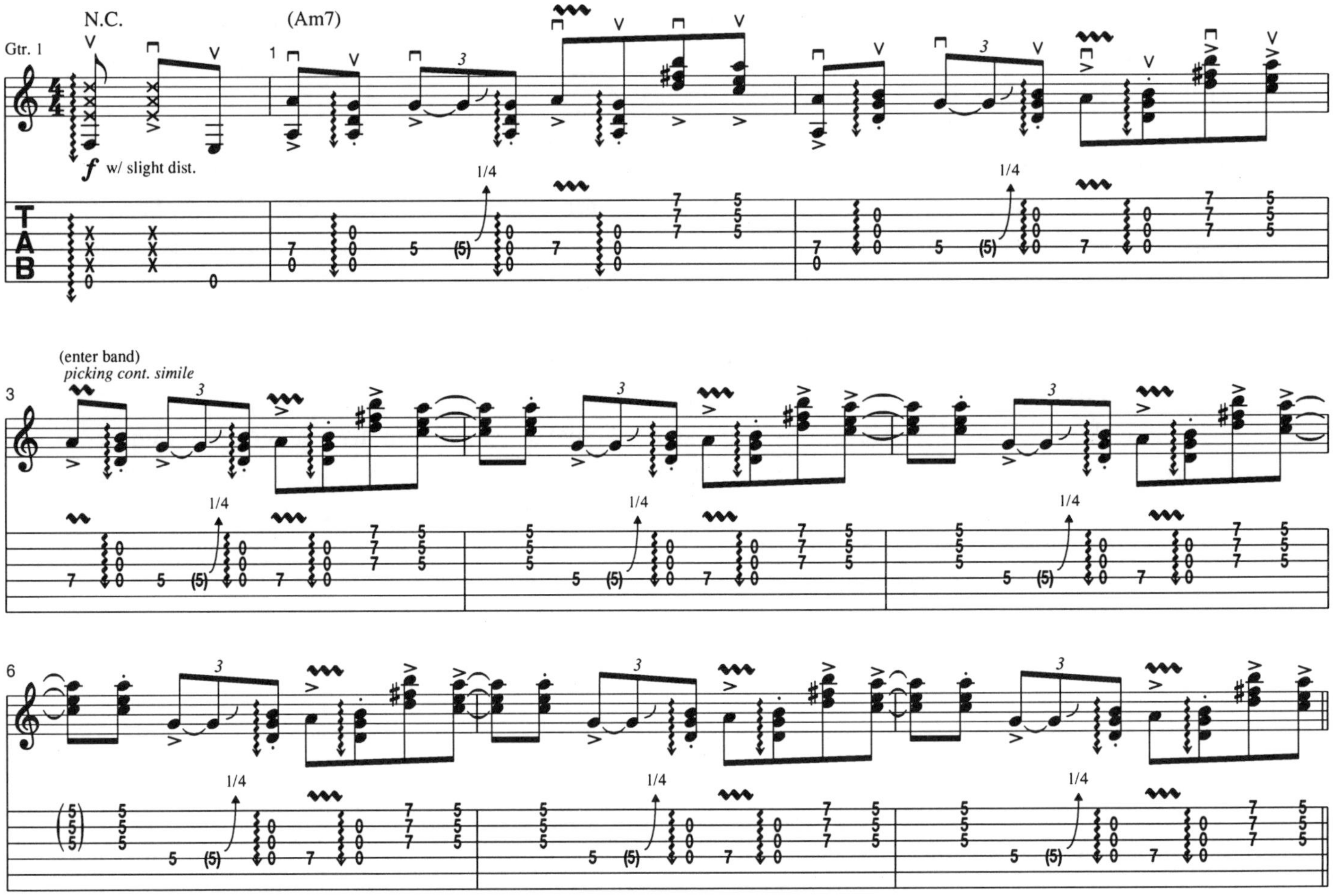

Figure 2 Study

This study consists of 17 measures and represents the first section of Stevie's solo. Note Stevie's use of triple stops and chords interspersed among the single note lines. This technique serves to remind the listener of the harmony and keeps things fresh and interesting as well.

Figure 2 Performance

The repetitive nature of "Cold Shot" despite its power and drive, would prove numbing if it was not for the unique arrangement.

The first part of the solo is constructed like a verse and chorus, save for the two measures of the im chord chopped off the end. This subtle alteration helps speed up the passage of time and sets the table for the sneaky second section of the solo.

The triple stop with a sliding bass note, found in beat 1 of measures 1 and 7 (over the im chord) and in beat 2 of measure 10 (over the ivm chord) can be a little tricky. It is played by using the index finger of the left hand to barre the top two strings (B and E) and the ring finger on the G string. As you strike the notes slide the ring finger up one fret while keeping the index finger in place. If this proves to be too difficult (if you have small hands), this lick can be accomplished by using the pinky on the left hand to hammer on the note, as opposed to sliding into it with the ring finger.

Figure 2
Guitar Solo

Figure 3 Study

Like a cat burglar, SRV quietly pussyfoots around with the arrangement in part two of the solo.

Fiqure 3 Performance

Ever the bluesman, even when acting cool in the sharkskin suit disguise of the funky soul man, Stevie Ray defiantly inserts a *12*-bar chorus of standard blues changes into the off-balance arrangement of "Cold Shot." Then, true to form, he harkens back to Big Albert the K for his muse. Born under a bad sign indeed!

Figure 3

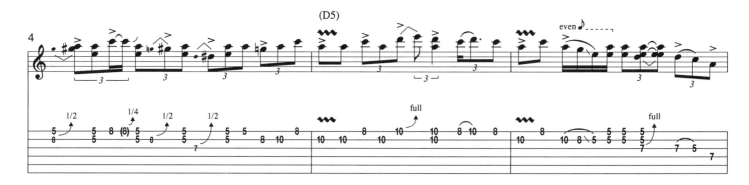

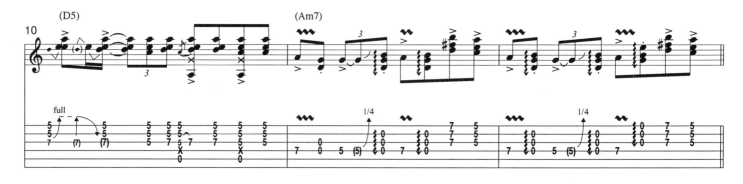

STANG'S SWANG
(Couldn't Stand the Weather)
Written by Stevie Ray Vaughan

From the sheen of sharkskin to the somber cut of formal attire, Stevie Ray changes hats and goes "Wes." In a classy tribute to both Mr. Montgomery and Kenny Burrell, "Stang's Swang" perfectly captures the ambience of the soulful, bluesy jazz presented by the Blue Note and Verve record labels in the fifties and sixties. Overtones of Grant Green, Irving Ashby, Eddie McFadden, and the young Pat Martino (with tenorist Willis "Gatortail" Jackson) are also heard.

"Chitlins Con Carne" by Kenny Burrell, "Comin' Home, Baby" by Herbie Mann, and "The Work Song" by Julian "Cannonball" Adderly are based on similar minor key progressions. By the way, Stevie forsook his treasured Strats for a big, fat Gibson Johnny Smith arch top guitar on this revved up retro cut.

Figure 1 Study

Letter B (the theme or "head") is sixteen measures long, containing im-IV-V chord changes and a bevy of substitutions.

Figure 1 Performance

The first eight measures are formed around a Gm7 (im) tonality, even though a quick D dominant (V7) substitute chord is slipped in for texture in measures 7 and 8. Measures 9-12 continue with the inferred Gm7 chord change.

The head is derived from the G blues scale (G-B♭-C-D♭-D-F) which functions nicely as a minor scale when played against a minor chord. In fact, the ♭3rd (B♭) and the ♭7th (F) illuminate the minor 7th tonality. Note the subtle use of the ♭5th (D♭) in measures 2, 6, 10, and 11. Jazz musicians are particularly fond of this scale degree as a bluesy dissonance and it has been described as the defining sound of post-War jazz. Adding authenticity to this period piece is Stan Harrison's tenor saxophone playing in unison with Stevie Ray in measures 1, 2, 4, 5, 6, 8, 9, and 10.

Measures 13-16 are an excellent introduction to the concept of "backcycling" and could be seen as another way to cover what would be V-IV-I-V chord changes in the last four measures of a standard 8- or 12-bar blues. A common compositional device is the cycle of 5ths, where chords follow each other in steps of five scale degrees apart in ascending order. For example: C-G-D-A-E-B-F♯-C♯ etc.. If you continued with the sequence, you would end up back at C! If you reverse direction, and move in 4ths (C-F-B♭-E♭-A♭ etc.) you will accomplish the same result. This is known as backcycling.

In measure 13 Stevie plays a C13 (the 4th of G) and continues backcycling until he gets to A♭13 in measure 15. Instead of following the A♭13 with its 4th, D♭13, he uses G13 as the *tritone-sub* of D♭13, thereby achieving the logical resolution to the root (G)! The interval of a tritone (a ♯4th, or ♭5th) exists in every dominant chord between the 3rd and ♭7th degrees. The formula for a D♭ dominant chord is D♭, F, A♭, C♭ (or B). For a G dominant it is G, B, D, F. Notice both chords contain F and B (or B and F), which are a ♭5th apart. The other two notes in each chord can be seen as altered tones from either the D♭ or G major scales. This concept, then, allows these chords to substitute for one other. Measure 16, naturally, resolves to the V (D) chord like most bluesy progressions.

Note that this sixteen-measure progression, like many others, could be viewed as *two* 8-bar sequences stitched together, each starting on the im and ending on the V7.

It should be made clear that Stevie Ray Vaughan was not a jazz guitarist. However, his exceptional skill and musical intuition enabled him to indulge his whims and pull off a respectable performance.

Figure 1

Tune Down 1/2 Step:
① = Eb ④ = Db
② = Bb ⑤ = Ab
③ = Gb ⑥ = Eb

SOUL TO SOUL
Epic FE 40036 (1985)

Just as Stevie looks cool and relaxed with his dot neck 335 on the cover, *Soul to Soul* is a more confident and laid back version of *Couldn't Stand the Weather*. It has the hot instrumental kicking off the show, the centerpiece slow blues extravaganza, the ripping Hendrix cover, and the slick jazz number. Four originals mix it up with two compositions by fellow Texan Doyle Bramhall and four hip remakes.

"Say What," "Ain't Gone 'N' Give Up on Love," "Empty Arms," and "Life Without You" are SRV creations that cruise from rock to blues and soul music. "Looking out the Window" and "Change It" groove through the auspices of Doyle Bramhall. Tastefully interwoven into the set are Hank Ballard's "Look at Little Sister," Eddie Harris's "Gone Home," Willie Dixon's "You'll Be Mine," and "Come On (Part III)," written by Earl King, but acquired by way of Jimi Hendrix.

Soul to Soul, while not lacking in excellent guitar adventures, shows a welcome slant towards great songs and arrangements. In addition, Stevie Ray's singing is more expressive and mature. With all this in mind, I have picked his "Ain't Gone 'N' Give Up on Love" and "Empty Arms," along with "Gone Home," to chart his musical development to 1985.

AIN'T GONE 'N' GIVE UP ON LOVE
(Soul to Soul)
Words and Music by Stevie Ray Vaughan

Stevie's ultimate tribute to Albert King, "Ain't Gone 'N' Give Up on Love," sounds like its inspiration was "Drowning on Dry Land" from King Albert's 1969 album *Years Gone By*. Like the majority of his work he adds the hefty stamp of his own personality. One of the more obvious ways in which he accomplishes this is through the insertion of a ten-measure bridge among the twelve-measure verses. His self-confident vocal while betraying "Bobby Blue" Bland as a major influence, tells a tale of sorrow that has the ring of truth.

Okay, let's saddle up and take this slow ride through Stevie and Albert's King-dom.

Figure 1 Study

The pick-up and four-measure intro are a succinct lesson in marking chord changes with common double stops and the skillful manipulation of the basic blues scale.

Figure 1 Performance

The pick-up is a variation on a double stop near and dear to Buddy Guy's heart. The index finger barres the top three strings while the ring and pinky handle the notes on the G string. As indicated in the notation this passage is played fingerstyle, with the right hand thumb plucking the G string simultaneously as the index plucks the high E.

Measure 1 proclaims the E dominant tonality with the D (♭7th) and B (5th) notes. Stevie Ray then anticipates the D9 (IV) chord in measure 2 by blurring the E (9th) and A (5th) notes together on the fourth beat of measure 1. The repeated bending of the D (root) up a full step to E (9th) in measure 2 keeps the D9 chord buoyant through to the A9 chord in measure 3, where the bend is followed by a pull-off from the D to the C (the 4th and ♭3rd in the key of A), resolving to the root (A).

Stevie sashays through the I-IV-I-V turnaround in measures 3 and 4 by emphasizing root (A) notes for the I (A) chord and the 5th (A), and the 9th (E) for the IV (D) chord. The V (E) chord is summarized with the root (E) bass note and the B\D double stop from measure 1.

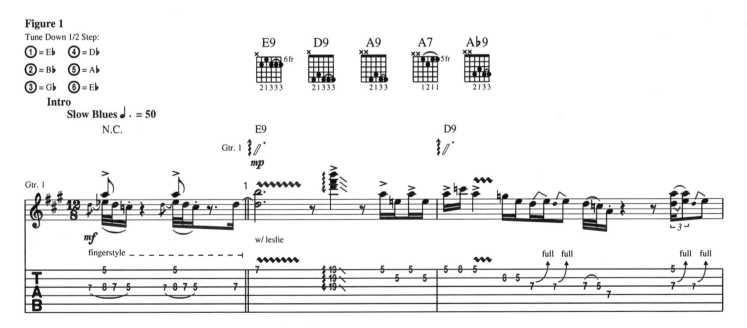

Figure 1

Tune Down 1/2 Step:
① = E♭ ④ = D♭
② = B♭ ⑤ = A♭
③ = G♭ ⑥ = E♭

E9   D9   A9   A7   A♭9

Intro
Slow Blues ♩. = 50

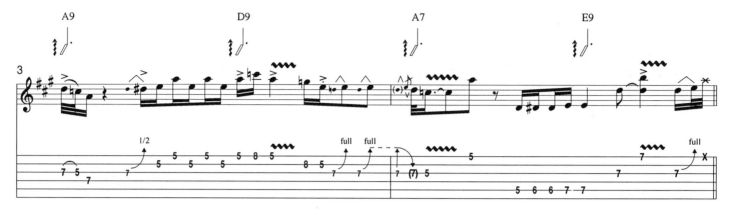

Figure 2 Study

The V and IV chords in measures 9 and 10 of verse one illustrate the power of a single note to imply a chord change.

Figure 2 Performance

With the invisible hand of Albert King to guide him, Stevie Ray curbs his tendency towards overstatement and identifies the V (E) and IV (D) chords with their respective 5ths (B and A). When played over the indicated E9 and D9 chords, the effect is bright and lyrical.

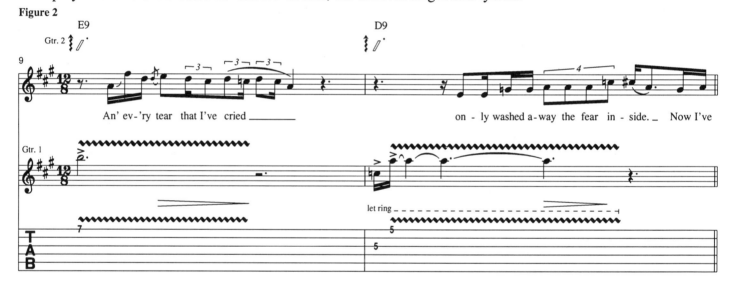

Figure 3 Study

The first 12 measures of the solo are a prime lesson in the art of string bending according to Mr. A. King. Of particular interest is the extensive use of the "Albert King box" at the eighth position.

Figure 3 Performance

Let us take this impressive string-choking exhibition measure by measure.

Measure 1 (I chord): A.K.'s classic 4th to 5th bend, resolving to the root (A), followed by the ♭3rd pushed to the 4th in anticipation of the IV chord in measure 2.

Measure 2 (IV chord): The 5th (A) of D is emphasized along with the bend from the ♭7th (C) to the root (D).

Measure 3 (I chord): With the vibratoed A note from measure 2 anticipating the I (A) chord in measure 3, the half-step bends from the ♭3rd (C) to the major 3rd (C♯) firmly identifying the chord change.

Measure 4 (I chord): After a definitive resolution to the root (A), Stevie Ray demonstrates a cascading series of half- and full-step bends that hit the 3rd (C♯), 4th (D), and 5th (E) degrees in the key of A.

Measure 5 (IV chord): With the tension being held up by the bend to the E (9th of D), the ♭7th (C) leading tone is chomped down on hard, followed by a subtle half-step bend of B (6th) to C. At this point for the first time in the solo, Stevie slips into the root position of the A blues scale at fret 5. He ends the measure with a bend from the root (D) to the 9th (E) before pulling off to the ♭7th (C) leading tone.

Measure 6 (IV chord): After a glancing blow to the 5th (A), Stevie repeatedly bends the root (D) to the 9th (E). On the last beat of the measure he vibratos the A (5th) in anticipation of the I (A) chord in measure 7.

Measure 7 (I chord): Stevie jumps right back on the D (4th) to E (5th) bend, maintaining the momentum from the previous measure.

Measure 8 (I chord): Heavy vibrato of the root (A) as a release (and relief) after all that gut-wrenching bending. Note the extremely cool sequence on the fourth beat, where the C (♭3rd) is bent a half step up to the C♯ (3rd), followed by the D (4th), nudged a quarter step before being pushed a full step to E (5th), in anticipation of measure 9.

Measure 9 (V chord): The C♯ (6th) is bent and vibratoed up to D (♭7th, leading tone) before the resolving bend up to E (root). The 4th (A) is heavily accented at the end of the measure, using the natural gravitation of this note (the root of the song) to move the ear towards the I chord in measure 1.

Measure 10 (IV chord): After a poignant vibrato of the 5th (A) at fret 10, Stevie hikes back down to the root position of the A blues scale at fret 5. During a brief visitation he wanks the root (D), to the 9th (E), before catching the 5th on the way to the I chord in measure 11.

Measures 11 and 12 (I, IV, I and V chords): With minimal outlining of the I-IV-I-V chords indicated in the turnaround, Stevie just drills the hell out of the root (A) in the root position of the A blues scale, one octave higher at fret 17. He does interrupt the insistent root note with the C (♭7th leading tone of D) at fret 20, bent a full step to D (root of IV chord) on beat three of measure 11. Likewise, he bends the C a half step to C♯ (3rd) for the first beat of measure 12 (I chord). On the last beat, he again bends the C up a full step to D, where it briefly functions as the ♭7th leading tone of the E (V) chord. The whole point is to maintain the drive of the solo as it continues into the next twelve-measure section. Stevie's solid sense of the chord sequence compels him to mark their passage with the appropriate notes.

Figure 3
  Guitar Solo

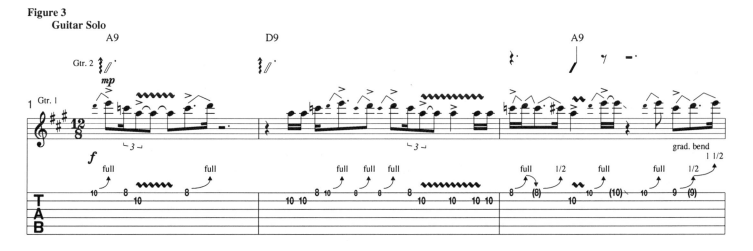

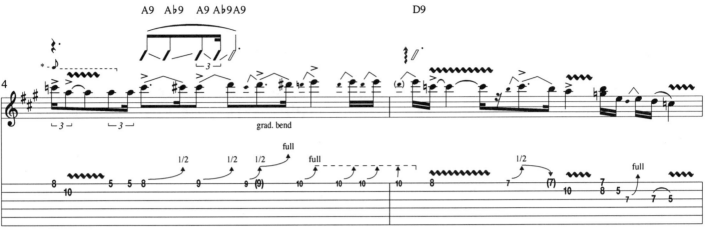

* Played behind the beat.

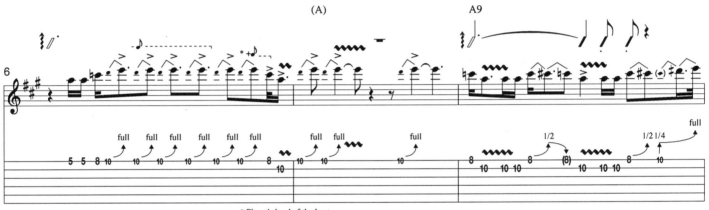

* Played ahead of the beat.

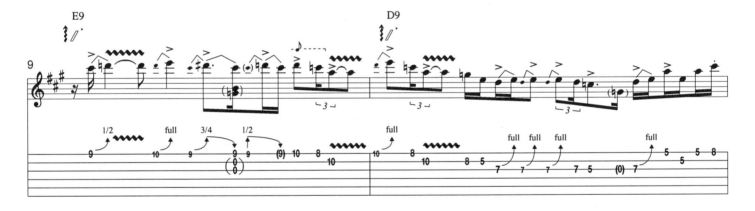

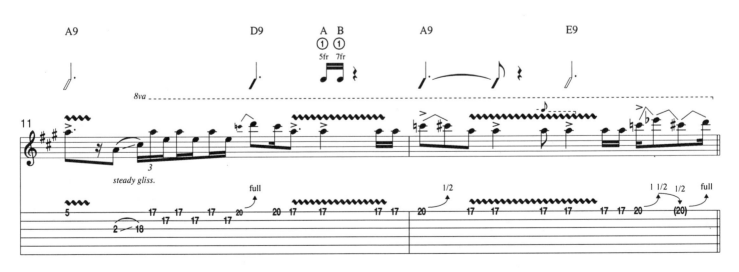

GONE HOME
(Soul to Soul)
Written by Eddie Harris

This swinging sample of soulful, sixties jazz performs the same function on *Soul to Soul* that "Stang's Swang" did on *Couldn't Stand the Weather*. Quite simply, it gives Stevie Ray a chance to make like Kenny Burrell or Grant Green for 3:04.

Tenor saxophonist Eddie Harris wrote this bluesy fingersnapper in 1961, the same year that he had a Top 40 hit with the movie theme from *Exodus*. He went on to have a commercially successful career doing more movie music, experimenting with electronic instruments in a jazz setting, and co-leading a group with Les McCann.

Stevie solos with more authority on "Gone Home" than "Stang's Swang." This could be the result of increased playing experience between the two albums, or more likely the fact that "Gone Home" is bluesier, with twelve-bar verses and I, IV, V chord changes.

After an eight-measure intro (that also acts as the interlude) derived from a D Mixolydian mode line played in unison by the guitar, organ, and bass, the arrangement consists of IV, I, IV, I, V, and I chord changes in the solos. The theme includes the IV chord after the V.

Figure 1 Study

The twelve-measure theme which is almost identical to Part I, is an eccentric pattern. It begins on the IV (G) chord for two measures, alternating with two measures of the I (D) chord for the first eight measures of the progression. From measures 9-12 it is standard blues changes of V, IV (one measure each), and I (two measures, with the rest in measure 12 implying a I chord).

Figure 1 Performance

The IV chord changes in measures 1-2 and 5-6 are basically the same pattern. Playing in the tenth position, Stevie infers a G dominant tonality with double stops in 6ths (D/F) and 5ths (D/G). These solid citizens of the G Mixolydian mode find their counterparts in the I-chord phrases (measures 3-4 and 6-7) where the root (D), 5th (A), and ♭7th (C) notes of the D Mixolydian mode mix it up with double stops in 3rds (B/G, A/F♯).

Measure 9 belies Stevie's "down home" blues roots with an ultra-hip run based on the "bebop seventh scale." This sophisticated variant on the Mixolydian mode contains the root, 2nd, 3rd, 4th, 5th, 6th, ♭7th, and the major 7th (usually a passing tone between the ♭7th and the octave). Over the V7 chord, SRV plays B (2nd), D (4th), F (♯5th, an altered tone), G♯ (7th), and A (root). Coolsville!

The venerable Mixolydian mode in the key of G appears in measure 10. A descending run of D (5th), C (4th), A (2nd), G (root), F (♭7th), and D (5th) identifies the IV chord, as well as looking ahead to the I (D) chord in measure 11.

Measure 11 proudly trumpets the blues with an implied IV-I change. The G6 (IV) adds musical tension, which is resolved to the I (D) with the hammer-on of the ♭3rd to the major 3rd on the G string while the 5th (D) is sustained on the B string.

Measure 12 is virtually a rest with a quick glissando from the ♯4th (G♯ in the key of D) connecting the inferred G9 triple stop in measure 1 of the organ solo that follows.

Figure 1

Tune Down 1/2 Step:
①= E♭   ④= D♭
②= B♭   ⑤= A♭
③= G♭   ⑥= E♭

Figure 2 Study

The first twelve measures of Stevie's solo once again demonstrates his skill at running I-IV-V chord changes. Nothing fancy here, just a good Texan playing bluesy Mixolydian mode licks.

Figure 2 Performance

<u>Measures 1 and 2 (IV chord)</u>: staying within the 13th and 10th (root) positions of the D blues scale, Stevie singles out the strong notes inferring a G dominant chord. These include the root (G), 4th (C), 5th (D), ♭7th (F) and 9th (A) notes that delineate the G Mixolydian mode in this context.

<u>Measures 3 and 4 (I chord)</u>: Here Stevie plays the ♭3rd (F) for spice, along with the major 3rd (F♯), root (D), ♭7th (C), and 4th (G) from the D hybrid blues/Mixolydian scale.

<u>Measures 5 and 6 (IV chord):</u> (see measures 1 and 2)

<u>Measures 7 and 8 (I chord):</u> Utilizing the D blues scale in the 13th position (the "Albert King box"), Stevie nails the 4th (G), ♭7th (C), and root (D) notes. In addition, on beat 2 of measure 8, he slips in the familiar ♭3rd-3rd-root classic blues lick. Only here it is on the high E and B strings, rather than the 10th position on the G and D strings.

<u>Measure 9 (V chord):</u> Here we find the root (A), 4th (D), and 9th (B) from the A Mixolydian mode.

<u>Measure 10 (IV chord):</u> Stevie plays the root (G), ♭7th (F) and 6th (E) from the G Mixolydian mode.

<u>Measures 11 and 12 (I chord):</u> Continuing the descending sequence of the root (G), ♭7th (F), and 6th (E) in the key of G from measure 10, measure 11 starts with the D (5th of G, but root of D in measures 11 and 12). The run further descends to the C (♭7th), A (5th), A♭ (♭5th) and G (4th). Measure 12 picks up the line at F (tangy ♭3rd), dropping to E (2nd) and finally resolving to D after a quick hit on that insistent "blue note," the ♭3rd (F).

Figure 2

49

EMPTY ARMS
(Soul to Soul)
Words and Music by Stevie Ray Vaughan

"Empty Arms" is a great, grooving Texas shuffle, one of Stevie's best compositions, and a tune that deserves to go on to become a blues standard. Stevie ended up being the *drummer*, as well as the singer and guitarist on this track when he and bassist Tommy Shannon were jamming in the studio during the *Soul to Soul* sessions and the engineer let the tape run. It is no surprise that he could play the drums so exceptionally, as every aspect of his guitar playing is heavily rhythmic. Be sure to check out the hard rockin' version of this cut on *The Sky Is Crying*. Besides being taken at a gallop instead of a trot, it sounds like a live studio recording, with no rhythm guitar overdubs or piano, as heard in this original version.

Figure 1 Study

The sliding 6-9 chords played by guitar 2 in the twelve-measure intro have a proud lineage that goes back to Johnny Moore. Moore was a pioneer electric blues and jazz guitarist who's Three Blazers backed up singer/pianist Charles Brown in Los Angeles in the late forties. His subtle and sensuous use of these blues forms became a signature of his style and has influenced scores of blues and jazz guitarists.

Figure 1 Performance

Play the D6-D9 shapes (Gtr. 2) in measures 1-4, 7, 8, 11, and 12 with your index, middle, and ring fingers on the G, D, and B strings, respectively. Play the G6-G9 and the A6-A9 shapes in measures 5, 6, and 9 with your index finger barring the top three strings. Note the close voicing between the D9 chord on beat 4 of measure 2 and the (inferred) G9 on beat 4 of measure 4. From "Rude Mood" on, Stevie showed sensitivity to efficient fingerings and the smooth transitions which they engender.

Guitar 1 in the twelve-measure intro is an excellent example of Stevie Ray taking Big Albert's bending and vibrato techniques, and forging them to fit his own musical sensibilities. The fluidity of his bent, sustained notes (along with his soprano sax-like tone) as well as the economy of execution, is a marvel to behold. Here is a measure by measure analysis of Stevie's performance.

Measure 1 (I chord): Here Stevie plays the 5th (A), 6th (B), root (D), and 9th (E, bent to F♯, the 3rd) from the D Mixolydian mode.

Measure 2 (I chord): A variation on the same phrase, with the F (♭3rd) bent a full step to G (4th), followed by the F bent a half step to F♯ (the major 3rd target note).

Measure 3 (I chord): Oh yeah! Stevie maintains the bend to the F♯ for three long beats, finally pushing it a half step more to G (4th) before resolving to the root (D) on the last eighth note of the measure. *Delicious* musical tension!

Measure 4 (I chord): The root (D) sustained from measure 3 is followed by the 9th (E) bent to F♯ (3rd).

Measure 5 (IV chord): The root (G) is bent up a full step to A (9th), followed by the F (♭7th leading tone) bent a full step to the root (G). The measure ends with resolution to the 5th (D), always a somewhat neutral tone.

Measure 6 (IV chord): The root (G) is bent a full step to the A (9th), followed by the kind of bend that separates the *real* bluesmen from the poseurs: a quarter-step bend from the ♭7th (F) to the micro-tone between the F(♭7th) and F♯ (major 7th in the key of G). Historically the micro-tone *between* the ♭7th and major 7th, not between the ♭3rd and major 3rd, has been called the "blue note." This is followed by resolution to the 5th (D) in anticipation of the I (D) chord in measure 7.

Measure 7 (I chord): The ♭3rd (F) cascaded into half- and full-step bends to the 4th (G). A welcome three beats separates a repeat of the ♭3rd bend into measure 8.

Measure 8 (I chord): A dip to that super cool quarter-step bend from the F (♭3rd), with the full bend next, resolving (at last) to the root (D). A sixteenth-note pull-off from C (♭7th) to A (5th) sets up the V (A) chord in measure 9.

Measure 9 (V chord): Licks from the D blues scale that suggest the V (A) chord. Stevie starts with the G (♭7th) bent a full step to the A (root), releasing it back to the G (♭7th). The same bend occurs again, ending on a quarter-step micro-tonal bend of the F (♯5th) taken from the A blues scale.

Measure 10 (IV chord): Repeated bending of the root (G) to the 9th (A), ending on the major 7th (F♯) of G. This happens to be the major 3rd target note of D—the chord change-coming up in measure 11!

Measure 11 (I chord): A quarter-step micro-bend from the 9th (A), resolving to the root (D). The measure ends with a chord embellishment involving a hammer-on from the ♭3rd (F) to the 3rd (F♯) while sustaining the B (6th) and C (♭7th), implying a D13 chord.

Measure 12 (I chord): Stevie doubles the D6 triple stop played by guitar 2. Notice the last note he plays is A (5th), even though the chord change is to the I (D), rather than the V (A). Force of habit? Who knows. At any rate guitar 3 completes *its* resolution to the root (D).

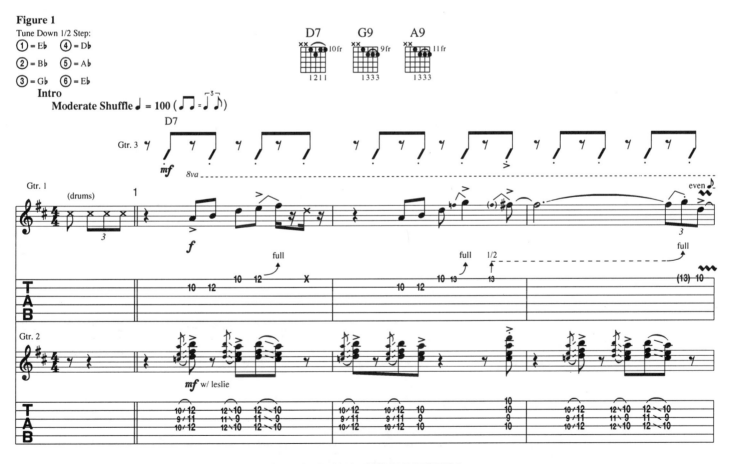

IN STEP
Epic OE 45024 (1989)

Ironically, *In Step* represented a series of firsts while tragically being Stevie Ray Vaughan's last album. It was the first and only release with Double Trouble he recorded substance-free, having undergone a period of rehab following *Soul to Soul* and *Live Alive*. It was also his only Grammy winner. However, the indomitable spirit that allowed him to rebound from rock bottom drug and alcohol despair could not prevent a helicopter from taking him down on August 27, 1990.

With his head clear, Stevie entered Kiva Studios in Memphis obsessed with getting his sound right. As a means to that end he filled the multi-level studio with *thirty-two* amps of all shapes and sizes. His aim was to record his solos through all thirty-two amps *simultaneously*, thereby giving himself the luxury of being able to choose the best tone later at the mix down. Cesar Diaz, the tube amp guru who teched on *In Step,* recalls the house rattling and humming from the aural onslaught. Stevie's .056 low E string had a particularly dramatic effect on the senses. After all was said (Stevie repeated like a mantra, "What's that?," whenever he would hear the studio walls sympathetically vibrating) and done (Cesar and his assistants running up and down the stairs to keep the amps operating properly—a logistical nightmare), a tweed 1959 Fender Bassman, with four ten-inch speakers, was used virtually for all the solos. Black face (pre-CBS) Fender Super Reverbs were employed for the rhythm tracks.

The results were spectacular; "The House Is Rockin'," the two instrumentals ("Travis Walk" and "Riviera Paradise") and the Doyle Bramhall co-authored "Tightrope," "Wall of Denial," and "Scratch-N-Sniff" showed Stevie's growth as a composer, as well as a virtuoso guitarist. "Crossfire" was penned by the Double Trouble rhythm section, while Willie Dixon's "Let Me Love You, Baby," Buddy Guy's "Leave My Girl Alone," and Wolf's "Love Me Darlin'" round out the set with Stevie's typically good taste in cover selection.

The funky soul of "Tightrope," the menacing slow blues of "Leave My Girl Alone," and the slashing shuffle blues of "Love Me Darlin'" are the stuff of legends, and our tunes of choice from *In Step.*

TIGHTROPE
(In Step)
Words and Music by Stevie Ray Vaughan and Doyle Bromhall

Stevie Ray's flair for odd-measured compositions is clearly demonstrated in "Tightrope." With I, IV, and V chords used individually and in concert with each other, eleven- and nine-measure verses nestle comfortably next to eight-measure choruses and twelve- and ten-measure solo sections. Combined with a four-measure intro and a twenty-eight-measure IV-I coda, he manages to make it look easy as he balances one part against another.

As do several other songs on *In Step,* "Tightrope" references Stevie's successful battle with substance abuse. Musically it looks back, as did "Couldn't Stand the Weather," to his early days when he played R&B and soul along with the blues. A sly allusion to James Brown is even made with the lyric "broke out in a cold sweat."

Figure 1 Study

Measures 1 and 2 of the intro function both as a hook and as a bridge to the chorus. Like the full intro, the two-measure phrase is usually repeated twice at the end of the verses. Note that Stevie truncates the second measure of the phrase at the completion of his solo before verse 3.

A comparison could be made between Figure 1 and the hook of Otis Redding's "Hard To Handle."

Figure 1 Performance

In measure 1 Stevie outlines the E chord with a root, 3rd, and 5th arpeggio. The D is indicated solely by the root and 3rd. The B7 chord is an actual four-note voicing.

Measure 2 finds an open A major chord followed by a G (root) note with octave Es, and an open position E blues scale lick, to complete the progression of E, D, B7, A, G, and E (7).

Figure 2 Study

The first twelve measures of the solo perfectly exemplify the new, improved Stevie Ray Vaughan. For a guy whose sound was never too shabby, he outdoes himself with *Eau de Tube Tone.* That combined with his clear focus, seems to have allowed him to have the confidence to play *less,* letting his phrases breathe next to each other. Of course, he still turned up the heat when he felt it was appropriate.

The B blues scale is employed to masterful effect at two positions throughout the entire solo.

Figure 2 Performance

Measure 1 (I chord): A very typical blues bend of the 4th (E) pushed to the 5th (F#) is followed by the same bend combined with the 5th and root. The bend is sustained before being released down into a classic 5th-3rd-root-♭7th blues phrase that resolves to the root in measure 2.

Measure 2 (I chord): The ♭3rd (D) is teased up a quarter step as it strives for the major 3rd (D#). Two pull-offs facilitate a descending run of the root, ♭7th, 5th, and 4th—an unusual note to end on over the I chord. A half-note rest adds drama to the bend from the ♭7th (A) to the root coming up in measure 3.

Measure 3 (I chord): After the bent, sustained and vibratoed root (B), another classic blues bend is proffered in dynamic contrast to the single sustained note. The root (B) on the high E string is followed by a bend on the G string of a 4th (E) to the 5th (F#). The T-Bone (through Chuck Berry) variation on this lick comes next with the 5th (F#) on the B string, added to the root to form a double stop of a 4th.

Measure 4 (I chord): After that (always) hip quarter-step bend from the ♭3rd comes a gliss from the root (B) on the B string and a G-string bend. This is followed by a 5th and root on the top two strings. A hammer/slide from the ♭7th (A) to the root on the B string, signals Stevie's move to the "Albert King box" for the IV chord in measures 5 and 6.

Measure 5 (IV chord): the 5th (B) and ♭7th (D) of E are alternately picked to imply an E dominant tonality, ending on that "blue note" of a quarter-step bend from the ♭7th.

Measure 6 (IV chord): more of the same (sans the non-notatable bend), with a bend from the root (octave) to the 9th (F#) to cement the E9 chord change.

Measure 7 (I chord): Stevie blends the "Albert King box" with the root position of the B blues scale. Roots and ♭7ths mingle with the ♭3rd (D) bent to the major 3rd (D#) target note—with the "blue note" *between* the ♭3rd and the 3rd snuck in to boot!

Measure 8 (I chord): more root position exploration, with an atypical (for Stevie) sustain on the ♭3rd. This stuff is pretty basic, but his phrasing is so logical and flowing (check out the note groupings of 3, 4, 3, 4) that he makes it sound fresh.

Measure 9 (I chord): Knowing full well the importance of signalling the pivotal V chord change in measure 9, Stevie starts compressing the sense of time after being so (relatively) expansive in the first eight measures. Again, he plays basic blues scale licks in the root position emphasizing the 5th (F#) and including the wonderfully expressive quarter-step bend from the ♭3rd. The steady sixteenth notes (save for the two *thirty -second* notes on beat four) set the table for the churning repetition in the next three measures.

Measures 10 (IV chord), 11, and 12 (I chord): Hang on to your hat! In the one virtuosic display during his solo, Stevie repeats a slurry, sixteenth-note lick of the 4th (E) bent up a full step to the 5th (F#), played against a double stop of a 5th, containing F# and D. Over the E (IV) chord this indicates the 9th and ♭7th. Over the I (B) chord, it infers the 5th and #9th. The tension and bluesy dissonance created by three measures of this wobbly-sounding lick is riveting as it charges ahead to the next section of the solo.

Figure 2

Guitar Solo

Figure 3 Study

Figure 3 begins several measures into the coda, and contains a double-string, double-stop bend of a full step that repeats over the IV-V vamp.

Figure 3 Performance

The wall of sound generated by this dizzying bend is stunning. The bent double stop of B/F♯ functions as the 5th and root of the I chord (B) and the 9th and 5th of the IV chord (E). However, the sonic effect of this repeated bending encompasses the A/F notes *and* the microtones that are glissed by on the way to the B/F♯.

I recommend playing the note on the B string with the pinky and the note on the G string with the ring finger (backed up by the middle finger). This will keep your hand in position to continue playing out of the root position of the B blues scale.

Figure 3

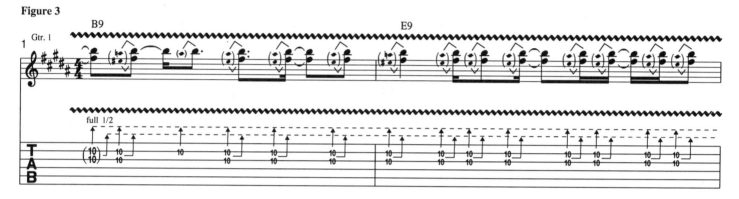

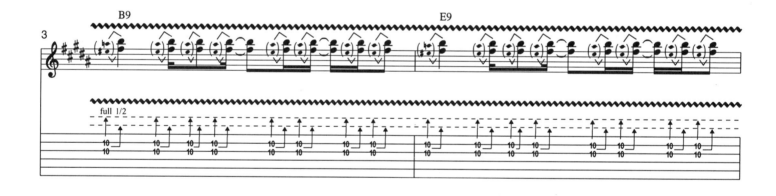

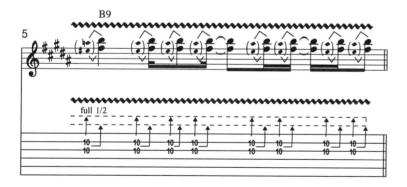

Figure 4 Study

Figure 4 which begins fourteen measures into the coda, contains a series of double-stop bends similar to Figure 3.

Figure 4 Performance

The full-step bend of D/A to E/B in measure 1 is harmonically speaking pretty much in the pocket. However, in measure 2 Stevie bends D#/A# (the major 3rd and 7th) up to F/C (the ♭5th and ♭9th) for a groovy, bluesy dissonance. Using this lick as a passing phrase, he quickly moves up a fret, bending E/B up a full step to F#/C#, inferring the 5th and 9th of B. He continues with this bend in measure 3 where the notes function as the 9th and 6th of E. These double-stop steps lead, quite satisfyingly, to a firm resolution on the B note at the end of the measure. Stevie then sustains the B into the next measure.

Figure 4

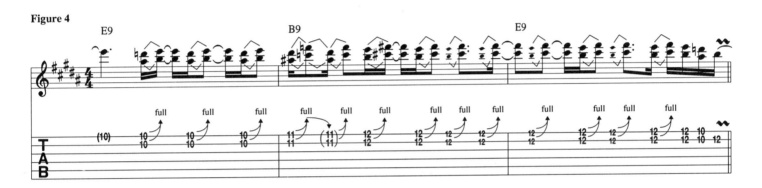

59

LEAVE MY GIRL ALONE
(In Step)
Words and Music by Buddy Guy

From *Left My Blues in San Francisco* (1967), Buddy Guy's first album for Chess Records, "Leave My Girl Alone" gives Stevie Ray a chance to fuse both Buddy's and Big Albert's approach with his own. Not to be overlooked is Stevie's powerful vocal on this slow blues classic. He sounds convincingly soulful and *threatening* at the same time—exactly what is called for in the reading of this tune.

Figure 1 Study

This is the first two measures of the intro. It is almost precisely like Buddy's original, reproduced repectfully by Stevie with a more legato feel.

Figure 1 Performance

The double-stop, hammer-on lick highlights the root (Bb) and b3rd (Db) from the Bb blues scale. The resolution to the F (5th) helps to infer the V chord change. The slurry bend on beat 4 of measure 2 is one of Buddy's patented tricks. As indicated, try it fingerstyle with your right thumb plucking down on the G string simultaneously as your index finger plucks the high E string. This may take some practice to coordinate the bending and releasing of the G string with your left hand.

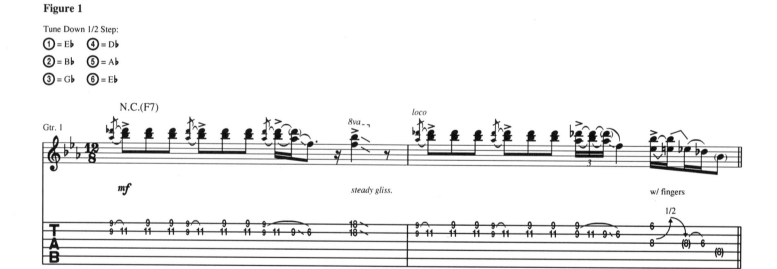

Figure 1

Tune Down 1/2 Step:
① = Eb ④ = Db
② = Bb ⑤ = Ab
③ = Gb ⑥ = Eb

Figure 2 Study

Figure 2 begins eight measures into the twelve-bar section of Stevie's solo. The upper register riffing is pure adrenalin, manifesting itself as musical expression.

Figure 2 Performance

<u>Measure 1 (I chord):</u> Playing in the root position of the B♭ blues scale *at the octave* (fret 18), Stevie fans the 5th (F) and root (B♭) notes. He then sneaks in some Mixolydian mode by including the C (9th, or 2nd) in conjunction with the ♭3rd (D♭), and ends the measure with a full-step bend of D♭ to E♭ (4th) as a prelude to measure 2 (V chord).

<u>Measure 2 (V chord):</u> A remarkable study in string control as Stevie combines the full-step bend from measure 1 (the ♭3rd to the 4th) with a half-step bend (the ♭3rd to the major 3rd). The resulting E♭ and E notes function as the ♭7th and major 7th in the key of F (V chord of B♭). Remember the real "historical" blue notes that we talked about earlier? By repeating the bend as a continuous loop, Stevie implies that "blue note," between the ♭7th and major 7th!

<u>Measure 3 (IV chord):</u> A series of licks in the root position of the B♭ blues scale (octave), with emphasis on the B♭ (5th of E♭) as anticipation of the I chord coming up in measure 4, and the 4th (E♭) bent a full step to F (5th). Combined in a double stop with the A♭ (♭3rd), a bluesy dissonance results that recalls B.B. King from his funky, fifties period.

<u>Measure 11 (I chord):</u> Stevie pounds home the root (B♭) note at the octave (fret 18), making a satisfactory resolution after three measures in the blue heavens.

Figure 2

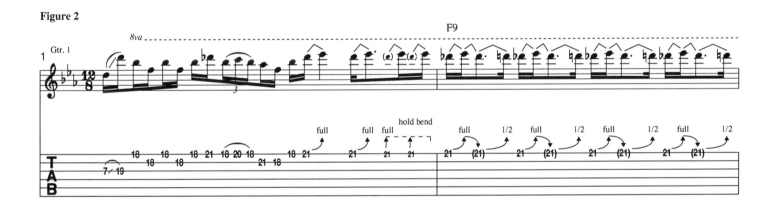

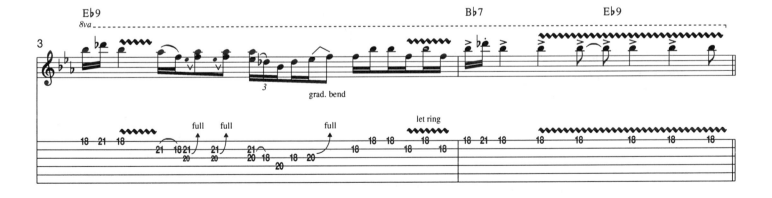

LOVE ME DARLIN'
(In Step)
Words and Music by Chester Burnett

Stevie Ray's wicked take on this Howlin' Wolf tune from 1964 shows a debt to one of his more obscure influences. With Buddy Guy playing rhythm on Wolf's original version, lead guitarist Hubert Sumlin wreaked havoc with *his* out-of-phase Strat, bending, slurring, and glissing with devilish abandon. Even a cursory listen to Hubert's work will show its hypnotic effect on Stevie.

"Love Me Darlin'" is a straight forward shuffle with standard twelve-bar changes. Using Hubert's ideas as a point of departure, Stevie rips and runs the 10-inch Jensen speakers in his tweed Bassman almost rattling out of their frames. "Love Me Darlin'" is one of his best blues covers, with snarling Texas tone and plenty of South Side attitude.

Figure 1 Study

This twelve-bar intro (with pick-up) shows once again how Stevie took inspiration from his legendary predecessors and fashioned it to fit his own estimable legacy.

Figure 1 Performance

Pick-up: One measure of the open D (4th) string, leading to the ♭3rd (B♭) on beat 4 serves as entry into measure 1. Of course, the 5th naturally resolves to the root.

Measure 1 (I chord): Stevie starts with a true "blue note" (the micro-tone between the ♭3rd and the major 3rd) before resolving to, and sustaining, the root (G).

Measure 2 (IV chord). That same blue note is followed by the 4th bent a full step to the 5th and landing on a double stop of a 4th (B♭/F, the ♭7th and 4th of C). The resolution is to the root (C) on beat 4.

Measure 3 (I chord): The ♭3rd (B♭) is bent a half step to B (3rd), with emphasis on the root (G) and piquant ♭3rd (B♭).

Measure 4 (I chord): Leaving some breathing space between his phrases (whew!), Stevie Ray harps on the 5th (D) and root (G).

Measure 5 (IV chord): A bend from the root (C) to the 9th (D) forecasts a spectacular bend, sustained through feedback, in measures 6-8. A vibratoed 5th (C) lies in counterpoint to the bend that precedes and follows it in measure 6.

Measures 6, 7, and 8 (IV and I chords): Soaring like a hawk silhouetted against the Texas sun, Stevie sustains through feedback the C (root), bent to D (9th), over the IV chord in measure 6, as well as the I chord in measures 7 and 8 (where the D functions as the 5th of G). On the fourth beat of measure 8 he releases the D down to C and plays the B♭ (♭3rd) in anticipation of the root (G) note in measure 9.

Measure 9 (V chord): The G (4th) is sustained, followed by root position riffing emphasizing the root (D) and 4th (G). The double stop of G/D (4th and root) anticipates the same double stop in measure 10.

Measure 10 (IV chord): More riffing in the root position, with the G/D double stop inferring the 9th and 5th of C. The root (C) is bent up a full step to the D (9th), helping to intensify the extended harmony (C9) over the indicated C7 chord.

Measure 11 (I chord): Resolution to the sustained and vibratoed root (G), with the blues scale used to spotlight the G/D double stop (5th and root) along with the ♭7th (F). A pull-off from the 4th (C) to the major 3rd (B) sets up the resolution back to the root for the first two beats of measure 12.

Measure 12 (V chord): The resolution to the root (G) in combination with a sweet bend of the ♭3rd (B♭) a full step to the 4th (C). Stevie completes the sequence with the final resolution to the 5th (D), functioning as the root of the V chord.

Figure 1

Tune Down 1/2 Step:

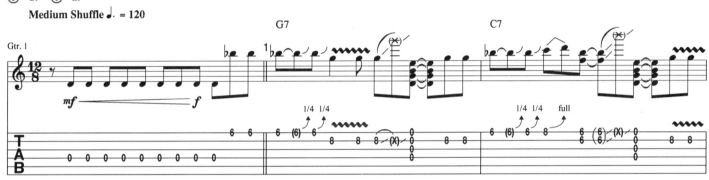

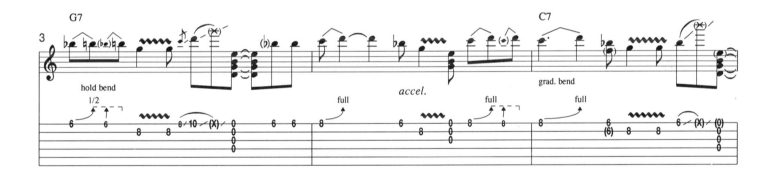

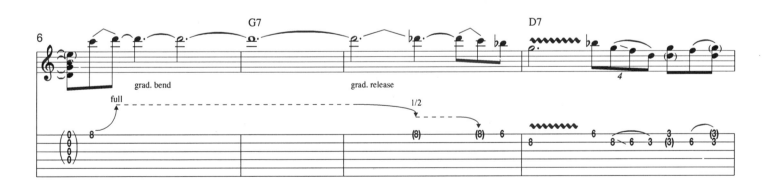

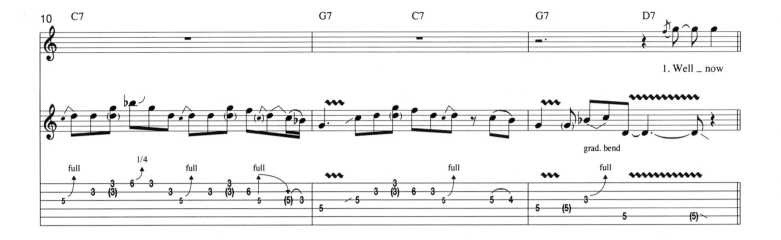

Figure 2 Study

Figure 2 is a classic Chicago blues fill, by way of Hubert Sumlin, that works particularly well over the I chord.

Figure 2 Performance

Using the root position of the G blues scale, Stevie starts with a bend of the ♭7th (F) to the root (G) on the B string, smacks the G/D double stop and then runs down the G blues scale from F to D to C (bent a full step to D) to C, ending with a nasty vibrato on the ♭3rd (B♭) as a tension note in anticipation of the next chord change.

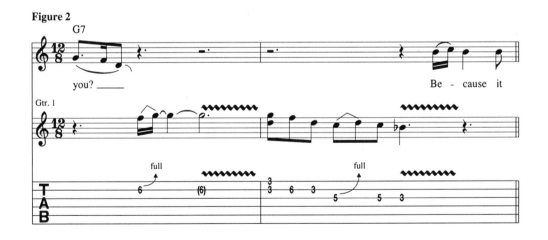

Figure 3 Study

Figure 3 is a similar phrase to Figure 2, but used as a turnaround, instead of a I chord fill.

Figure 3 Performance

After a brutish double-stop mash of F/C♯ to G/D, Stevie plays almost exactly the same run as Figure 2. However, instead of ending on the ♭3rd (B♭) he adds the G, bends the B♭ a half step to B (major 3rd) to nail the I chord, then resolves to the 5th (D).

THE SKY IS CRYING
(Epic 47390 (1991)

This posthumously released recording contains ten tracks waxed between *Couldn't Stand the Weather* (1984) and *In Step* (1989). The selections represent material that was not included, for various reasons, on the studio albums during that period of time. A reprise of "Empty Arms" (taken at a much brisker tempo than on *Soul to Soul*), "So Excited," and the acoustic "Life By The Drop" are the only original compositions. "Boot Hill," "The Sky Is Crying," "Little Wing," "Wham," "May I Have a Little Talk with You," "Close To You," and "Chitlins Con Carne" were all favorite covers of Stevie Ray and Double Trouble that were regularly performed live. Following a familiar and winning approach, a Hendrix classic ("Little Wing"), a jazz standard (Kenny Burrell's "Chitlins Con Carne") and a smoking instrumental ("So Excited") round out a set of traditional blues.

I have opted for "So Excited" as the object of our inspection from *The Sky Is Crying*.

SO EXCITED
(The Sky Is Crying)
Written by Stevie Ray Vaughan

The bass line that propels "So Excited" has its genesis in tunes like Ray Sharpe's "Linda Lu," Buddy Guy's "I Got My Eye on You," and the Yardbirds' "Got to Hurry."

With the repetition of its hooky bass line, this number is a natural for Stevie Ray to do his "rhythm and lead thing" as he darts in and out of the pattern with licks and fills.

It is fitting the last song in this book is a trio piece, probably recorded live in the studio, by a modern master of the genre.

Figure 1 Study

The first four measures (I chord) of letters A (theme), D (main riff) and H (main riff) illustrate Stevie's highly developed sense of rhythmic variation on a theme. It may have been entirely intuitive, but it worked. His attention to the rhythmic details sets him apart from most of his contemporaries and is one of the major lessons that can be learned from a study of his music.

Figure 1 Performance

The one-measure increment for "So Excited" is a bass line played in swing eighths (and in a 12/8 time signature), consisting of the root on beat one, the octave on beat two, the ♭7th on beat three and the 5th on beat four. It moves from the I to IV to V chord changes with the same relative notes.

For the purposes of our examination, let us look at each measure in terms of the four beats that Stevie phrases on and around.

A Theme

Measure 1: On beat 1 Stevie bends the 4th (D) to the 5th (E). On beat 2 he plays the A/E double stop of a 4th, sustaining it through beats 3, 4, *and* beat 1 of measure 2.

Measure 2: Beat 2 contains the open D (4th) and G (♭7th) strings and the fretted D bent up to E. Stevie sustains the bend over to beat 3 where he adds the ♭3rd (C) bent a "blue note" quarter step. Beat 4 has the root (octave) and the ♭7th (G).

Measure 3: Stevie swings pairs of eighth notes for three beats, playing three eighth notes on beat 4. He follows the bass pattern closely for the first three beats, playing a double stop of E/C (♭3rd and 5th) on beat 4.

Measure 4: Once again he is close to being rhythmically and melodically in sync with the bass. He has the root and octave on the first two beats, but he plays the ♭3rd (in place of the ♭7th) on beat 3 and a pull-off from the 4th to the ♭3rd (instead of the 5th) on beat 4.

D Main Riff

Measure 1: Beat 1 is the double stop of E/C for the duration of an eighth note, paired with a quarter-note rest. Beat 2 is the tonic while beat 3 is the ♭7th for an eighth note in conjunction with a quarter-note rest. Beat 4 is a quarter-note rest with an A9/C♯ chord for an eighth note.

Measure 2: The A9 chord is sustained across the bar line for an eighth note, along with the open D and G strings, for beat 1. Beat 2 (as usual) is the tonic while beat 3 is the ♭7th. Beat 4 is the 5th on the A string and the triple stop of C, E, and A on the top three strings.

Measure 3: Beat 1 is a quarter-note rest with two sixteenth notes—the first a D (4th) note and the second a muted strum! Beat 2 is the double stop of D/A and the tonic. Beat 3 is the ♭7th and beat 4 is a quarter-note rest with a triple stop of a ♭7th, 9th, and 5th, suggesting an A9 chord.

Measure 4: Beat 1 is a quarter-note rest with the open D, G, and B strings. Beat 2 is the tonic, beat 3 the ♭7th, with beat 4 echoing measure 2.

H Main Riff

Measure 1: Stevie rests on beat 1, plays the root on beat 2, the ♭7th on beat 3, and the 4th bent to the 5th on beat 4.

Measure 2: The release of the 5th from measure 1 is played, combined with the ♭3rd and root (octave) takes care of beat 1. Beat 2 consists of a quarter-note rest and the root for the duration of an eighth note. Beat 3 has the ♭7th and beat 4 has the 5th on the A string paired with the bent 5th (octave) on the G string!

Measure 3: Beat 1 is the released 5th (down to the 4th) from measure 2 along with the ♭3rd. Beat 2 is a quarter-note rest with the tonic as an eighth note. Beat 3 is the ♭7th and beat 4 has the same lick as measure 2.

Measure 4: Beats 1, 2, and 3 are the same as measure 3. Beat 4 is the open A string and octave A paired with a triple stop containing the ♭3rd, 5th, and root, on the top three strings.

Figure 1

Tune Down 1/2 Step:
① = E♭   ④ = D♭
② = B♭   ⑤ = A♭
③ = G♭   ⑥ = E♭

D **Main Riff**

H **Main Riff**

Guitar Notation Legend

Guitar Music can be notated three different ways: on a *musical staff*, in *tablature*, and in *rhythm slashes*.

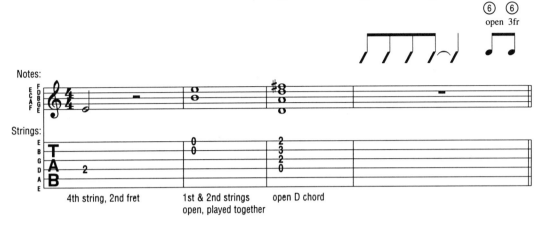

RHYTHM SLASHES are written above the staff. Strum chords in the rhythm indicated. Use the chord diagrams found at the top of the first page of the transcription for the appropriate chord voicings. Round noteheads indicate single notes.

THE MUSICAL STAFF shows pitches and rhythms and is divided by bar lines into measures. Pitches are named after the first seven letters of the alphabet.

TABLATURE graphically represents the guitar fingerboard. Each horizontal line represents a a string, and each number represents a fret.

Definitions for Special Guitar Notation

HALF-STEP BEND: Strike the note and bend up 1/2 step.

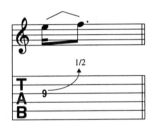

WHOLE-STEP BEND: Strike the note and bend up one step.

GRACE NOTE BEND: Strike the note and bend up as indicated. The first note does not take up any time.

SLIGHT (MICROTONE) BEND: Strike the note and bend up 1/4 step.

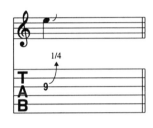

BEND AND RELEASE: Strike the note and bend up as indicated, then release back to the original note. Only the first note is struck.

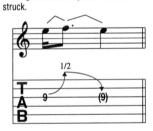

PRE-BEND: Bend the note as indicated, then strike it.

PRE-BEND AND RELEASE: Bend the note as indicated. Strike it and release the bend back to the original note.

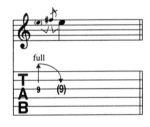

UNISON BEND: Strike the two notes simultaneously and bend the lower note up to the pitch of the higher.

VIBRATO: The string is vibrated by rapidly bending and releasing the note with the fretting hand.

WIDE VIBRATO: The pitch is varied to a greater degree by vibrating with the fretting hand.

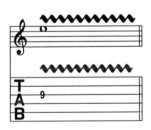

HAMMER-ON: Strike the first (lower) note with one finger, then sound the higher note (on the same string) with another finger by fretting it without picking.

PULL-OFF: Place both fingers on the notes to be sounded. Strike the first note and without picking, pull the finger off to sound the second (lower) note.

LEGATO SLIDE: Strike the first note and then slide the same fret-hand finger up or down to the second note. The second note is not struck.

SHIFT SLIDE: Same as legato slide, except the second note is struck.

TRILL: Very rapidly alternate between the notes indicated by continuously hammering on and pulling off.

TAPPING: Hammer ("tap") the fret indicated with the pick-hand index or middle finger and pull off to the note fretted by the fret hand.

NATURAL HARMONIC: Strike the note while the fret-hand lightly touches the string directly over the fret indicated.

PINCH HARMONIC: The note is fretted normally and a harmonic is produced by adding the edge of the thumb or the tip of the index finger of the pick hand to the normal pick attack.

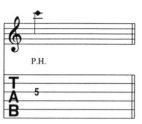

HARP HARMONIC: The note is fretted normally and a harmonic is produced by gently resting the pick hand's index finger directly above the indicated fret (in parentheses) while the pick hand's thumb or pick assists by plucking the appropriate string.

PICK SCRAPE: The edge of the pick is rubbed down (or up) the string, producing a scratchy sound.

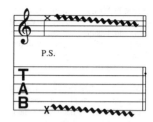

MUFFLED STRINGS: A percussive sound is produced by laying the fret hand across the string(s) without depressing, and striking them with the pick hand.

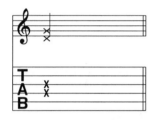

PALM MUTING: The note is partially muted by the pick hand lightly touching the string(s) just before the bridge.

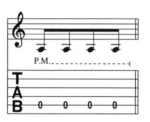

RAKE: Drag the pick across the strings indicated with a single motion.

TREMOLO PICKING: The note is picked as rapidly and continuously as possible.

ARPEGGIATE: Play the notes of the chord indicated by quickly rolling them from bottom to top.

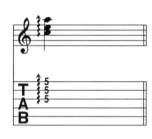

VIBRATO BAR DIVE AND RETURN: The pitch of the note or chord is dropped a specified number of steps (in rhythm) then returned to the original pitch.

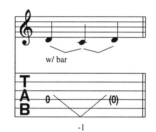

VIBRATO BAR SCOOP: Depress the bar just before striking the note, then quickly release the bar.

VIBRATO BAR DIP: Strike the note and then immediately drop a specified number of steps, then release back to the original pitch.

Additional Musical Definitions

(accent) • Accentuate note (play it louder)

(accent) • Accentuate note with great intensity

(staccato) • Play the note short

⊓ • Downstroke

V • Upstroke

D.S. al Coda • Go back to the sign (𝄋), then play until the measure marked "**To Coda**," then skip to the section labelled "**Coda**."

D.S. al Fine • Go back to the beginning of the song and play until the measure marked "**Fine**" (end).

Rhy. Fig. • Label used to recall a recurring accompaniment pattern (usually chordal).

Riff • Label used to recall composed, melodic lines (usually single notes) which recur.

Fill • Label used to identify a brief melodic figure which is to be inserted into the arrangement.

Rhy. Fill • A chordal version of a Fill.

tacet • Instrument is silent (drops out).

• Repeat measures between signs.

| 1. | 2. | • When a repeated section has different endings, play the first ending only the first time and the second ending only the second time.

NOTE: Tablature numbers in parentheses mean:
1. The note is being sustained over a system (note in standard notation is tied), or
2. The note is sustained, but a new articulation (such as a hammer-on, pull-off, slide or vibrato begins, or
3. The note is a barely audible "ghost" note (note in standard notation is also in parentheses).

RECORDED VERSIONS

The Best Note-For-Note Transcriptions Available

ALL BOOKS INCLUDE TABLATURE

00690002 Aerosmith – Big Ones $22.95
00694909 Aerosmith – Get A Grip $19.95
00692015 Aerosmith's Greatest Hits $19.95
00660133 Aerosmith – Pump $19.95
00694865 Alice In Chains – Dirt $19.95
00660225 Alice In Chains – Facelift $19.95
00694925 Alice In Chains – Jar Of Flies/Sap $19.95
00694932 Allman Brothers Band – Vol. 1 .... $24.95
00694933 Allman Brothers Band – Vol. 2 .... $24.95
00694934 Allman Brothers Band – Vol. 3 .... $24.95
00694826 Anthrax – Attack Of The Killer B's $19.95
00694876 Chet Atkins – Contemporary Styles $19.95
00694877 Chet Atkins – Guitar For All Seasons $19.95
00694918 The Randy Bachman Collection $22.95
00694929 Beatles: 1962-1966 .... $24.95
00694930 Beatles: 1967-1970 .... $24.95
00694880 Beatles – Abbey Road $19.95
00694832 Beatles For Acoustic Guitar $19.95
00660140 Beatles Guitar Book $19.95
00690044 Beatles – Live At The BBC $22.95
00694891 Beatles – Revolver $19.95
00694914 Beatles – Rubber Soul $19.95
00694863 Beatles – Sgt. Pepper's Lonely Hearts Club Band $19.95
00694931 Belly – Star $19.95
00694884 The Best of George Benson $19.95
00692385 Chuck Berry $19.95
00692200 Black Sabbath – We Sold Our Soul For Rock 'N' Roll $19.95
00694770 Jon Bon Jovi – Blaze Of Glory $19.95
00690008 Bon Jovi – Cross Road $19.95
00694871 Bon Jovi – Keep The Faith $19.95
00694775 Bon Jovi – Slippery When Wet $19.95
00690102 Bon Jovi – These Days $19.95
00694935 Boston: Double Shot Of Boston $22.95
00694762 Cinderella – Heartbreak Station $19.95
00692376 Cinderella – Long Cold Winter $19.95
00692375 Cinderella – Night Songs $19.95
00694875 Eric Clapton – Boxed Set $75.00
00692392 Eric Clapton – Crossroads Vol. 1 .... $22.95
00692393 Eric Clapton – Crossroads Vol. 2 .... $22.95
00692394 Eric Clapton – Crossroads Vol. 3 .... $22.95
00690010 Eric Clapton – From The Cradle $19.95
00660139 Eric Clapton – Journeyman $19.95
00694869 Eric Clapton – Unplugged $19.95
00692391 The Best of Eric Clapton $19.95
00694896 John Mayall/Eric Clapton – Bluesbreakers $19.95
00694873 Eric Clapton – Timepieces $19.95
00694837 Albert Collins – The Complete Imperial Recordings $19.95
00694862 Contemporary Country Guitar $18.95
00660127 Alice Cooper – Trash $19.95
00694941 Crash Test Dummies – God Shuffled His Feet $19.95
00694840 Cream – Disraeli Gears $19.95
00690007 Danzig 4 .... $19.95
00694844 Def Leppard – Adrenalize $19.95
00660186 Alex De Grassi Guitar Collection $19.95
00694831 Derek And The Dominos – Layla & Other Assorted Love Songs $19.95
00660175 Dio – Lock Up The Wolves $19.95
00660178 Willie Dixon $24.95
00694920 Best of Free $18.95
00690089 Foo Fighters $19.95
00690042 Robben Ford Blues Collection $19.95
00694894 Frank Gambale – The Great Explorers $19.95
00694807 Danny Gatton – 88 Elmira St $19.95
00694848 Genuine Rockabilly Guitar Hits $19.95
00694798 George Harrison Anthology $19.95
00690068 Return of The Hellecasters $19.95
00692930 Jimi Hendrix – Are You Experienced? $19.95
00692931 Jimi Hendrix – Axis: Bold As Love $19.95
00694944 Jimi Hendrix – Blues $24.95
00660192 The Jimi Hendrix – Concerts $24.95
00692932 Jimi Hendrix – Electric Ladyland $24.95
00694923 Jimi Hendrix – The Experience Collection Boxed Set $75.00
00660099 Jimi Hendrix – Radio One $24.95
00694919 Jimi Hendrix – Stone Free $19.95
00660024 Jimi Hendrix – Variations On A Theme: Red House $19.95
00690017 Jimi Hendrix – Woodstock $24.95
00690038 Gary Hoey – Best Of $19.95
00660029 Buddy Holly $19.95
00660200 John Lee Hooker – The Healer $19.95
00660169 John Lee Hooker – A Blues Legend $19.95
00690054 Hootie & The Blowfish – Cracked Rear View $19.95
00694905 Howlin' Wolf $14.95
00694850 Iron Maiden – Fear Of The Dark $19.95
00694938 Elmore James – Master Electric Slide Guitar $14.95
00694833 Billy Joel For Guitar $19.95
00660147 Eric Johnson $19.95
00694912 Eric Johnson – Ah Via Musicom $19.95
00694911 Eric Johnson – Tones $19.95
00694799 Robert Johnson – At The Crossroads $19.95
00693185 Judas Priest – Vintage Hits $19.95
00660050 B. B. King $19.95
00690019 King's X – Best Of $19.95
00694903 The Best Of Kiss $24.95
00690070 Live – Throwing Copper $19.95
00694954 Lynyrd Skynyrd, New Best Of $19.95
00694845 Yngwie Malmsteen – Fire And Ice $19.95
00694756 Yngwie Malmsteen – Marching Out $19.95
00694755 Yngwie Malmsteen's Rising Force $19.95
00660001 Yngwie Malmsteen's Rising Force – Odyssey $19.95
00694757 Yngwie Malmsteen – Trilogy $19.95
00694956 Bob Marley – Legend $19.95
00690075 Bob Marley – Natural Mystic $19.95
00694945 Bob Marley – Songs Of Freedom $24.95
00690020 Meat Loaf – Bat Out Of Hell I & II $22.95
00694952 Megadeth – Countdown To Extinction $19.95
00694951 Megadeth – Rust In Peace $22.95
00694953 Megadeth – Selections From "Peace Sells... But Who's Buying?" & "So Far, So Good...So What!" $22.95
00690011 Megadeath – Youthanasia $19.95
00694868 Gary Moore – After Hours $19.95
00694849 Gary Moore – The Early Years $19.95
00694802 Gary Moore – Still Got The Blues $19.95
00690103 Alanis Morissette – Jagged Little Pill $19.95
00694958 Mountain, Best Of $19.95
00694895 Nirvana – Bleach $19.95
00694913 Nirvana – In Utero $19.95
00694901 Nirvana – Incesticide $19.95
00694883 Nirvana – Nevermind $19.95
00690026 Nirvana – Unplugged In New York $19.95
00694847 Best Of Ozzy Osbourne $22.95
00694830 Ozzy Osbourne – No More Tears $19.95
00694855 Pearl Jam – Ten $19.95
00693800 Pink Floyd – Early Classics $19.95
00693864 Police, The Best Of $18.95
00694967 Police – Message In A Box Boxed Set $70.00
00692535 Elvis Presley $18.95
00690032 Elvis Presley – The Sun Sessions $22.95
00694975 Queen – Classic $24.95
00694974 Queen – A Night At The Opera $19.95
00694969 Queensryche – Selections from "Operation: Mindcrime" $19.95
00694910 Rage Against The Machine $19.95
00693910 Ratt – Invasion of Your Privacy $19.95
00693911 Ratt – Out Of The Cellar $19.95
00690055 Red Hot Chili Peppers – Bloodsugarsexmagik $19.95
00690090 Red Hot Chili Peppers – One Hot Minute $22.95
00690027 Red Hot Chili Peppers – Out In L.A. $19.95
00694968 Red Hot Chili Peppers – Selections from "What Hits!?" $22.95
00694892 Guitar Style Of Jerry Reed $19.95
00694899 REM – Automatic For The People $19.95
00694898 REM – Out Of Time $19.95
00660060 Robbie Robertson $19.95
00694959 Rockin' Country Guitar $19.95
00690014 Rolling Stones – Exile On Main Street $24.95
00694976 Rolling Stones – Some Girls $18.95
00694897 Roots Of Country Guitar $19.95
00694836 Richie Sambora – Stranger In This Town $19.95
00694805 Scorpions – Crazy World $19.95
00694916 Scorpions – Face The Heat $19.95
00694870 Seattle Scene $18.95
00690076 Sex Pistols – Never The Bollocks, Here's The Sex Pistols $19.95
00690041 Smithereens – Best Of $19.95
00694885 Spin Doctors – Pocket Full Of Kryptonite $19.95
00694962 Spin Doctors – Turn It Upside Down $19.95
00694917 Spin Doctors – Up For Grabs $19.95
00694921 Steppenwolf, The Best Of $22.95
00694801 Rod Stewart, Best Of $22.95
00694957 Rod Stewart – Unplugged...And Seated $22.95
00690021 Sting – Fields Of Gold $19.95
00694824 Best Of James Taylor $16.95
00694846 Testament – The Ritual $19.95
00694887 Thin Lizzy – The Best Of Thin Lizzy $19.95
00690030 Toad The Wet Sprocket $19.95
00694410 The Best of U2 .... $19.95
00694411 U2 – The Joshua Tree $19.95
00690039 Steve Vai – Alien Love Secrets $24.95
00660137 Steve Vai – Passion & Warfare $24.95
00694904 Vai – Sex and Religion $24.95
00690023 Jimmy Vaughan – Strange Pleasures $19.95
00690024 Stevie Ray Vaughan – Couldn't Stand The Weather $19.95
00694879 Stevie Ray Vaughan –In The Beginning $19.95
00660136 Stevie Ray Vaughan – In Step $19.95
00660058 Stevie Ray Vaughan – Lightnin' Blues 1983 – 1987 .... $24.95
00690036 Stevie Ray Vaughan – Live Alive $24.95
00694835 Stevie Ray Vaughan – The Sky Is Crying $19.95
00690015 Stevie Ray Vaughan – Texas Flood $19.95
00690025 Stevie Ray Vaughan – Soul To Soul $19.95
00694776 Vaughan Brothers – Family Style $19.95
00660196 Vixen – Rev It Up $19.95
00694789 Muddy Waters – Deep Blues $24.95
00690071 Weezer $19.95
00694888 Windham Hill Guitar Sampler $18.95

Prices and availability subject to change without notice. Some products may not be available outside the U.S.A.

For More Information, See Your Local Music Dealer, Or Write To:

HAL•LEONARD

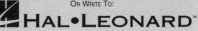

guitar SCHOOL

Guitar School takes you to class when it comes to learning how your favorite artists play. Every book comes complete with lessons on the guitar techniques and styles that make that artist special. Solos, riffs and all relevant guitar parts are discussed in the lessons, followed by exact transcriptions of these parts in both notes and tab. If you want to improve your chops, this series provides you with special exercises and lesson books by experts in the field. All books include tablature.

Beatles Guitar Techniques
Not only is this a stylistic analysis of the guitar licks and solos of the Beatles, but a deeper study of John, Paul and George's individual guitar concepts and techniques. A wonderful chronological sampling of early and later Beatles material is covered, complete with lessons and details on the Beatle who actually played the guitar parts. A must for anyone wanting an inside look at the Beatles' songs.
00660105 ....$19.95

Eric Clapton Solos
with lessons by Jesse Gress
This *Guitar School* book contains lessons with transcriptions of the solos to Eric Clapton's best work. It helps you understand as well as play the music. Includes 16 of his best, including: After Midnight (2 versions) • Lay Down Sally • Cocaine • Strange Brew.
00660088 ....$14.95

Best Of Def Leppard
This book takes you on a guided tour through the guitar styles of Def Leppard, showing the development of the Def Leppard sound. It includes lessons with theory and style information to help you incorporate the concepts behind these styles into your own playing. Includes licks from 12 classics, including: Bringin' On The Heartbreak • Love Bites • Pour Some Sugar On Me • Photograph • and more.
00660333...$16.95

Al DiMeola Solos
by Dan Towey
This exploration of DiMeola's music includes transcribed solos, lessons, and 17 songs: Adonea • The Embrace • Global Safari • Indigo • Kiss My Axe • Last Tango For Astor • Morocco • One Night Last June • Ritmo De La Noche • Traces Of A Tear • and more.
00660336...$14.95

In Deep With Jimi Hendrix
In Deep With Jimi Hendrix brings you closer to the music and the artist than you've ever imagined. This is accomplished through breaking down and reassembling the solos, riffs, rhythm figures, harmony lines, ensemble parts, and more. All performance techniques and equipment are explored in detail. If you want to learn the techniques of Hendrix, this is the book for you.
00660335...$16.95

Jimi Hendrix Solos
with lessons by Dave Whitehill
13 songs from this legend, including: All Along The Watchtower • Castles Are Made Of Sand • Foxy Lady • Hey Joe • Little Wing • Purple Haze.
00660086 ....$12.95

Eric Johnson
This book explores twelve tracks from Eric's two solo albums *Tones* and *Ah Via Musicom*. Transcription excerpts are provided with accompanying lessons on how to perform and study the playing techniques involved in each example.
00695002...$14.95

Judas Priest – Hell Bent For Lead Licks
Complete with full analysis of over 50 Priest licks. Other highlights include an exclusive interview with both K.K. Downing and Glen Tipton about their unique sound and style, a complete discography and and track-by-track breakdown of their guitar solos cross referenced with the Hal Leonard *Judas Priest Recorded Versions* folios.
00660089...$16.95

Kiss: Featuring The Guitar Styles of Ace Frehley & Paul Stanley
A master class teaching all of the essential licks and tricks by Kiss guitarists Ace Frehley, Paul Stanley, and more. Featuring songs like "Shout It Out Loud" and "Love Gun."
00696547...$16.95

Yngwie J. Malmsteen – Transcribed Solos
This book contains lessons with transcriptions in notes and tab of 14 of Yngwie Malmsteen's latest best solos. Dave Whitehill's instruction helps you understand as well as play the music.
00660090...$14.95

Guitar School Presents Gary Moore
Here's an in-depth look at the guitar style of the modern rock master. From his days with Thin Lizzy through his current blues-based explorations, you'll follow the evolution of the Gary Moore style. Includes transcriptions of excerpts from many of Gary's best recordings in notes and tab, along with lessons on the techniques used.
00660332...$16.95

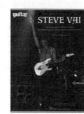

Guitar School Presents Steve Vai
Learn nearly every technique in Steve Vai's incredible arsenal, including speed picking, whammy bar usage, exotic scales, tapping, harmonics, rhythms, and more! This book features instructions and tips as well as transcriptions in notes and tab of songs like "Touching Tongues," "For The Love Of God," and "The Animal."
00660025...$16.95

Stevie Ray Vaughan: Big Blues From Texas
by Dave Rubin
Learn the hottest licks and rhythms selected from Stevie Ray's greatest songs. Each song is explained and analyzed through in-depth lessons and transcriptions. This information will not only allow access to Stevie's music, but will also inspire you to create your own improvised solos. 15 songs, including: Pride And Joy • Scuttle Buttin' • Empty Arms • Love Struck Baby • and more.
00660045...$16.95

Prices, content, and availability subject to change without notice

FOR MORE INFORMATION, SEE YOUR LOCAL MUSIC DEALER, OR WRITE TO:

HAL•LEONARD™ CORPORATION
7777 W. BLUEMOUND RD. P.O. BOX 13819 MILWAUKEE, WI 53213

0496